The Death Railway in Numbers

The Death Railway in Numbers

The Human Tragedy of the Thailand-Burma Railway in WW2

John Grehan

FRONTLINE BOOKS

First published in Great Britain in 2026 by
Frontline Books
An imprint of Pen & Sword Books Limited
Yorkshire – Philadelphia

ISBN 978 1 03619 201 3

A CIP catalogue record for this book is available from the British Library.

Typeset by Mac Style
Printed in the UK by CPI Group (UK) Ltd, Croydon, CR0 4YY.

MIX
Paper | Supporting responsible forestry
FSC® C013604
FSC www.fsc.org

The Publisher's authorised representative in the EU for product safety is Authorised Rep Compliance Ltd., Ground Floor, 71 Lower Baggot Street, Dublin D02 P593, Ireland.
www.arccompliance.com

For a complete list of Pen & Sword titles please contact:

PEN & SWORD BOOKS LIMITED
47 Church Street, Barnsley, South Yorkshire, S70 2AS, England
E-mail: enquiries@pen-and-sword.co.uk
Website: www.pen-and-sword.co.uk
or
PEN AND SWORD BOOKS
1950 Lawrence Road, Havertown, PA 19083, USA
E-mail: uspen-and-sword@casematepublishers.com
Website: www.penandswordbooks.com

Contents

Introduction

A faint, shrill sound penetrated the lush, tangled jungle, subduing the screech of exotic birds and the chatter of unseen monkeys. Growing slowly louder it formed into a distinct rhythm, and then the unmistakeable strains of 'Colonel Bogey' whistled by a battalion of ragged but proudly disciplined, khaki-clad British soldiers who marched into view. This is one of the most memorable scenes of the ever-popular movie *The Bridge On The River Kwai*. Perhaps surprisingly, this, or something very similar, did indeed really happen in March 1942 when British troops marched into Tamarkan camp to start work on the famous bridge at Kanchanaburi.

Though much of what was subsequently shown in the film was pure fiction, the suffering and ill treatment endured by the prisoners compelled to work on the Thailand to Burma railway was all too disturbingly real.

While the reminiscences and documented accounts of the deprivation, the degradation and starvation the POWs endured paint vivid pictures of man's inhumanity to man, nothing can compare with the stark reality of numbers. Stripped of false memories, untainted by time, figures are facts.

Drawn predominantly from official documents and reports, many produced during the period of construction and operation of the railway, *The Death Railway in Numbers* is supplemented by diaries compiled secretly and at great risk to the diarists and is enlivened by the recollections of survivors. The resultant statistics of this dreadful episode reveal both the magnitude of the task that was undertaken and the extent of the suffering of those compelled to work and live in conditions almost too horrifying to conceive. Sobering, shocking, often surprising, interpret them as you will, the truth lies in the numbers.

I must express my gratitude to Andrew Snow of The Thailand-Burma Railway Centre, Kanchanaburi, for all his support and guidance, and to Robert Mitchell who helped with the illustrations for this book.

John Grehan
Lancing
West Sussex
May 2025

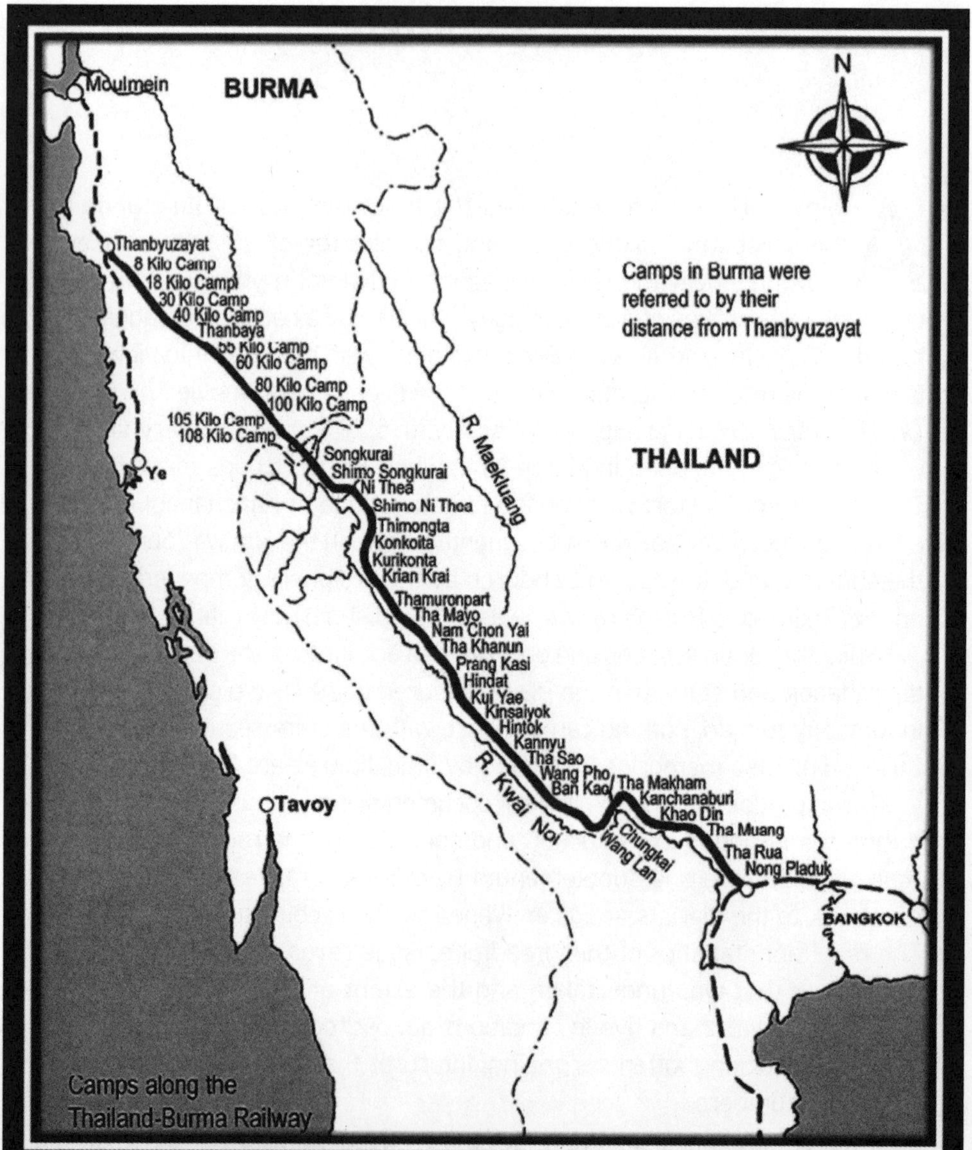

Map showing the route of the railway. (*Australian-Thailand Chamber of Commerce 2006*)

Chapter 1

The Plan

485 On 20 June 1942, orders were issued from Tokyo for the construction of a railway that would link the existing rail networks of Thailand and Burma. It was completed on 17 October 1943, **1** year, **3** months and **28** days later – **485** days.

16 is how many days between the issuing of the orders to build the railway and for Britain to be aware of it. A message from the Japanese Foreign Minister in Tokyo to the Japanese Ambassador was intercepted on 6 July. It read, in part: 'I have already telegraphed to the Army that I should like a railway built between [some point in Thailand] and Panhon [Japanese phonetics] in Burma for purely military use. I said that I should like the military to negotiate with Thailand for this, in fulfilment of Article 4 of the Japan-Thailand military agreement, and that as far as possible it was not to be a diplomatic negotiation ...'My intention is that the Army should build the railroad with Japanese materials but with Thai labour, and though I wish them to gain the cooperation of the Thais in expropriation of land, engagement of coolies, and so on, they must see to it that the cost is all paid for by themselves and that the Thais have no expenses. Further, this railroad is to be entirely for military use, but if it became unnecessary in the future to use it as an Army railroad, I feel it is difficult to give any commitment now as to whether we would dismantle it or else negotiate with the Thais to make it a leased or a jointly run railroad.'[1]

2218 This is the distance in nautical miles from Bangkok to Rangoon by sea. Overland, it is a little over **500** miles. That the Japanese would wish to shorten the time it would take to supply its front in northern Burma is obvious. It is normally stated that the reason the Japanese decided to build the Thailand-Burma railway was because they were suffering heavy losses to their merchant marine from the attacks of US submarines – and that was certainly a factor, as the Japanese conceded themselves – but they had planned to link the two countries by rail long before Pearl Harbor. If, as Japanese Imperial General Headquarters anticipated, their forces occupied Thailand and Burma, such a rail link would be an entirely sensible infrastructure development.

1885

Such a development had already been considered and in this year British colonial surveyors first looked at linking together the rail networks of Burma and Thailand. The route regarded as the most practicable was that from Moulmein in Burma to Phitsanulok in Thailand – much shorter than the one adopted by the Japanese in 1942. The scheme was abandoned because, among other reasons, it was though it would cost too many lives in its construction and maintenance. The Japanese also carried out a survey in the 1920s and then, in 1939, Japanese Imperial Headquarters, in anticipation of occupying Thailand and Burma in the future, undertook an assessment of which routes might be most practical for a railway which would link the two countries. In all, **5** routes were considered with the one which ran from Kanchanaburi in Thailand to Thanbyuzayat in Burma being that selected.

Starting at Non Pladuk this route was to follow the Mae Klong river to Tamarkan where the river splits into two tributaries; the railway was to follow the north-west tributary, the Khwae Noi, continuing across the frontier to the Three Pagodas Pass.

In Burma, it would descend along the course of the Zami and Airan rivers for a distance, then proceed on, following various small steams to Thanbyuzayat.

The route was to traverse laterally the formidable Bilauktbung range of mountains which forms the natural boundary between the two countries, as well as the Taungmyo range in Burma. **70** per cent of the route was to pass through thick malaria-infested jungle. The terrain was precipitous and, in many places, solid rock would have to be hewn though and hundreds of streams and dry gaps would have to be bridged.

This was in fact one of the oldest trade routes in that part of the world. According to local legends the area was far more densely populated in the past and Burmese warriors used to sail down from the north to loot central Siam. Such raids, it is suggested, were the reason the natives abandoned the region. The ancient occupation of the area was confirmed by the discovery of dozens of Palaeolithic artifacts in the area of Ban Kao POW camp in 1943 by Hendrik Robert van Heekeren, an appointed Dutch Prehistorian for the Archaeological Survey of the Netherlands East Indies, while working on the railway. He was assigned to the nail crew, which had to drive wire nails into the sleepers, which gave him the opportunity to dig into the ground and uncover the artifacts.[2]

In anticipation of the order to go ahead with the project, in January 1942, Major General Fukube of the Japanese Southern Army's No.2 Railway Control had begun surveying the route. He estimated it would take **2** years to build what was officially called the 'Thai Burma Rail Link' along the chosen route. It was also estimated that the project would require the employment of **60,000** labourers.

2 The railway was to be built by **2** Imperial Japanese Army railway regiments. The 5th Railway Regiment was given the task of constructing the line in Burma, with its base in Thanbyuzayat, and the 9th had the job of building the line in Thailand, its base being in Kanchanaburi. Both of these came under the 2nd Railway Administration Department. At full war strength, a Japanese railway regiment consisted of **83** officers, **271** non-commissioned officers, and **2,196** other ranks covering all the different trades and skills. There were also special bridging units, a materials workshop, a signals unit, a labour unit and specialist civilian engineers.[3] Altogether, there were in the region of **1,100** men at the workshop in Kanchanaburi which was capable of handling **500** trucks/cars a year and could cope with the maintenance/repair of **12** locomotives simultaneously. It had **3** forges, **3** engine shops. **1** foundry, **3** power stations, **1** saw mill, **1** water conduit, and an installation for refining crude oil.[4] The gauge of the railway was to be **1** metre.

13,000

The total number of Japanese involved in the project amounted to around **13,000**. This included a number of additional units transferred to help advance progress on the railway during the rushed construction known as the 'speedo' period. These were, the 4th Auxiliary Railway Unit, the 41st Independence Garrison Infantry Battalion, the Imperial Guards Railway Regiment, the 54th Engineer Regiment, the 42nd Line of Communication Area Unit, the Field Construction Service Unit of the 14th Division, the main part of the Epidemic Prevention and Water-supply Depot of the South Army, and the Field Hospital of the 21st Division.[5]

The main part of the 1st Railway Material Depot was deployed in Nong Pladuk and the other part in Rangoon. There was also a Railway Inspection Office. The two ends of the line would meet at the Thail-Burmese border by the Three Pagodas Pass, **897** feet above sea level.

Due to the need for the railway to be built quickly, construction began before the route had been fully surveyed. This proved to be self-defeating as the route eventually taken was not the most suitable one on which to build a railway and necessitated cutting through the Tenasserim Hills – one section of which was labelled by the POWs 'Hellfire Pass' – and surmounting difficult stretches, such as the Wampo viaduct. The lack of a thorough survey of the route manifested itself in other ways, such as too-steep gradients and unnecessary curves which had to be corrected after the completion of the railway.[6]

The intention was that the materials for the construction of the railway would be found locally, supplemented where necessary with items from the Japanese home islands. Food provision and its storage for those working on the construction was the responsibility of the 42nd Commissary Area Unit and of the Yoshikawa Butai. The former was to supply meat and vegetables and the latter rice, salt, sugar and other condiments.[7]

The building of the railway came under the command of Major General Shinoda, who was the Chief Inspector of the Second Railway Inspection Office. However, in January 1943 Shinoda was killed when his aeroplane crashed into a mountain on the Thailand-Burma border during an inspection of the railway. Also killed in the same crash was Major Irie, the chief of staff of the construction operation.

3,000

This was the original projected transport capacity in tons of the railway per day in each direction. This was later modified to **1,000** tons and even that was never achieved.

100,000,000

A sum of **100** million yen was allocated to the project.

¼

A quarter of all the steel rails for the track would be sent from Japan, the remaining three-quarters was to be dismantled by the Japanese from tracks in Malaya and Burma. The greater part of the workshop equipment was to come from Malayan tin mines. The remainder came from railway workshops at Kuala Lumpur, Java and Sumatra. Only a very small proportion was sent from Japan.[8]

For the building of the railway a large labour force was required, and this would have to be imported as the territory through which the line was to be built was very sparsely populated. Fortunately for the Japanese a very large body of men had fallen into their hands. Japanese successes in the early months of the war had led to the capture of significant numbers of British, Australian, Indian, Netherlands and United States servicemen. Approximately **130,000** Allied troops surrendered to the Japanese at the Fall of Singapore which marked the end of the Malayan campaign. Of these **38,496** were British troops and **16,701** were Australians. The number of Indian Army soldiers who were taken prisoner was **67,340** in addition to **14,382** local volunteer troops.[9] Around **45,000** of the Indian troops were persuaded to join the Japanese-sponsored Indian National Army instead of facing internment.

1

Of all these men one man in particular stood out. This was the only soldier to be awarded the Victoria Cross during the disastrous Malay campaign. Lieutenant Colonel Charles Groves Wright Anderson was in command the 2/19th Battalion of the Second Australian Imperial Force (2nd AIF). The citation for his VC explains, in part, how he was sent with a small force 'to restore a vital position and to assist a Brigade. His Force destroyed ten enemy tanks. When later cut off, he defeated persistent

Lieutenant Colonel Charles G. W. Anderson was the only Allied soldier to be awarded the Victoria Cross during the Malay Campaign of 1941–2 which resulted in the capture of the British and Australian troops who were forced to work on the Thailand-Burma railway.

attacks on his position from air and ground forces and forced his way through the enemy lines to a depth of fifteen miles. He was again surrounded and subjected to very heavy and frequent attacks resulting in severe casualties to his Force. He personally led an attack with great gallantry on the enemy who were holding a bridge and succeeded in destroying four guns. Lieutenant Colonel Anderson, throughout all this fighting, protected his wounded and refused to leave them. He obtained news by wireless of the enemy position and attempted to fight his way back through eight miles of enemy occupied country. This proved to be impossible, and the enemy were holding too strong a position for any attempt to be made to relieve him.'[10] Anderson took command of one of the groups of prisoners sent to work on the railway. Anderson Force, as it became known, comprised of **750** men and was shipped to Burma in October 1942.

Most of the prisoners of war were initially held in Singapore's Changi Gaol. This was not one camp but rather a collection of up to **7** internee camps, occupying an area of approximately **25** square kilometres. Its name came from the peninsula on which it stood, at the east end of Singapore Island.

An analysis of the labour statistics would indicate that roughly **118,000** labourers, both POWs and *rŏmusha* (a 'paid conscripted labourer', usually referred to by the prisoners as 'coolies') were brought into the construction area before the end of 1942. They were offered six-month contracts, though these were rarely honoured, and they were usually kept working until they died or were permanently crippled.

The manner in which many of these men were conscripted was described by the Labour Superintendent of Burmese Coolies: 'They had been arrested in the streets, near the river, on the market square and in the stations, marched off to labour camps and virtually kept as prisoners. They belonged to all classes of the population and they had left their villages, unknown to their families. As a direct consequence many civilians left their houses and fled from these districts, afraid to be abducted by the Japanese.'[11] Many managed to escape on the way to the work camps. The Labour Superintendent estimated that around **7,000** never reached the work camps and a further **2,000** escaped from the work camps soon after they arrived, while **300** died and **2,700** fell sick. As a result, the Japanese ordered another batch of conscripts to be found. A further **30,000** were collected but rumours of the conditions they would be subjected to had spread, and of these **10,000** escaped before reaching Thanbyuzayat. Again, of this second batch more than **3,000** died and others escaped, leaving only about **8,000** to work on the railway.

At the time they were rounded up, they were told they would receive free food, housing, clothing and medical care as well as compensation for their families if they died during their period of work on the railway. This never happened as no proper records were kept by the Japanese.

When the pace of the work on the railway was increased in 1943, a call was made for a further intake of native workers. Many volunteered at the prospect of a regular income and free food. Conditions in Malaya under Japanese rule had deteriorated with no work and rice having become scarce. Normally, the natives in Malaya ate **1.5** pounds of rice a day but they had only been able to obtain **8** pounds a month.[12]

More precise figures were compiled by the Deputy Director of Labour in the Japanese sponsored Burmese Provisional Government. He stated that in total **177,300** were demanded by the Japanese but only **110,346** were rounded up. Of these, **37,845** escaped on route to Moulmein and a further **7,621** escaped from Moulmein. Another **1,167** arrived in such a poor shape they were unfit for work. This means that of the **177,300** the Japanese wanted, only **20,321** were put to work on the railway.[13]

10 is the number of work forces assembled by the Japanese from the Allied prisoners and sent to assist the Japanese war effort.

Of these, **6** were to work on the railway. The 1929 Geneva Convention permits the employment of POWs on work of a non-military nature and the Japanese justified their employment on the railway because 'this construction was partly work to be done far from the front and partly bore the mission of the trade route between Thailand and Burma'.[14]

These were 'A' Force of **3,000** men, all of who were Australians, which was sent to Burma, initially to construct airfields and then to work on the railway, under the command of Brigadier Arthur Varley. It was organised into three battalions known by the name of their respective commanders – Major C. E. Green of the 2/4th Machine Gun Battalion, Lieutenant Colonel George Ramsay, and Lieutenant Colonel C. M. Black. 'A' Force was the first large body of POWs to be moved from Singapore to Burma. They were transported in two old ships, *Celebes Maru* and *Tohohasi Maru*. Brigadier Varley wrote in his diary about the congestion of the men in ships' holds where diarrhoea and dysentery were widespread and the latrines utterly inadequate. 'As we had rain daily and nightly we had to sit up in our capes to keep bodies dry. Little sleep obtained, all things getting wet.' The men in the holds were forced to crouch on temporary decks with head room of only about **1.2** metres. Adding to the prisoners' discomfort was that **2** landing barges were placed across the top of the holds blocking almost all sunlight.

Their situation deteriorated even further on *Celebes Maru* when **350** Japanese troops embarked, pushing the POWs further into the bottom of the hold where, Lieutenant Colonel Ramsay reported, 'the conditions were appalling'. The temperature in the holds never dropped below **100** degrees Fahrenheit so some of the prisoners slept in the coal bunker, preferring to endure the incessant rain they were exposed to.

'B' Force of **1,487**, was sent to Borneo to construct airfields. 'C' Force, of **551** prisoners, was sent to Japan to work in shipyards, factories and mines. 'D' Force, of **2,780** British and **2,220** Australians, was sent to Eastern Thailand to work on the railway, and 'E' Force, of **500** men, was sent to Borneo also to

A convoy carrying members of 'F' Force to Singapore station on the first leg of their terrible journey deep into the jungles of Thailand. (AWM P02569.174)

construct airfields. Other groups were formed to work on the railway when it was realised that the line would not be completed in the required time, including, in May 1943, 'F' Force and 'H' Force which were sent to work on the railway, and these included a large number of men who were in poor physical shape. The **2,340** British and **660** Australians of 'H' Force had been put together from POW holding camps in Singapore and Java, while 'F' Force was composed of prisoners held in Singapore's Changi gaol, many of whom had been considered too old or unwell to undertake heavy manual labour. 'K' and 'L' forces were sent to Thailand to provide medical services to the Asian labourers. The former was under the command of British Major E. E. D. Crawford, was made up of **230** medical staff **163** British, **55** Australian **11** Dutch and one other national. 'K' Force left Singapore on 24 August 1943 led by Lieutenant Colonel H. C. B. Benson RAMC and was made up of **42** British and **73** Australians.

27 This was the space in inches allowed for each man in the accommodation huts which from June 1942 began to be built by small parties of prisoners sent into Thailand ahead of the main work parties. The huts followed a standard pattern. They were generally **80** to **100** metres long with king-post trusses at approximately **3**-metre intervals so that the hut was divided into sections known as bays. Into each section as many as **20** prisoners were packed. Arthur Godman described these huts which he first saw at Ban Pong: 'The walls were made of woven palm leaves called bertam; this is a palm tree that grows in swamps and produces leaves that are quite stiff when dried and broad enough to be woven into a wall. The roof was made of atap, another type of palm tree with narrow leaves that are bent round a bamboo cane case which is about four feet long. Layers of these attaps are tied to the rafters with an upper atap projecting over a lower one, to form a thatched roof, which provides good protection against heat and rain. Along each was a low platform of bamboo called a chung ...These bamboos are beaten flat and then beaten again to remove the nodes of the stems ...The flattened bamboos were laid as a low platform, about six inches high, on either side of the hut, backing on to the wall. This left a passage way of about four feet.'[15] **Shortly after these initial groups arrived at the site of the camps the main working parties followed.**

32 is how many prisoners on average were packed into rice trucks as the POWs forming the working parties were taken by train from Singapore to Thailand. Adrian Kannegieter, a junior seaman with the Royal Netherlands Navy, was one of those who experienced that journey: 'The waggons were completely covered with metal sheets, which became as hot as a furnace at midday, when the sun was at its hottest. The men were packed in cars that were too small to hold about thirty each. Cramped on the floor, trying not to touch the hot metal sheets, the journey became an ordeal. Smoke and soot from the engine penetrated the waggons. And during the whole trip, the train regularly stopped for hours in the blazing sun, to let opposing trains pass, the railroad being a single track. At night lying on the floor was quite impossible. Dysentery excretions, urine and sweat made the atmosphere inside the carriages unbearable.'[16]

Examples of the trucks the prisoners were transported in can be seen today at the Hellfire Pass Memorial. The actual measurement of these was 16 feet x 7 feet 6 inches.

A rare toilet stop for the prisoners on one of the trains from Changi to Bam Pong in Thailand. (*AWM P02569.184*)

British prisoner John Barnard described what he said was the worst journey he had ever undertaken: 'The days were worse than the nights. The heat blazed down on the steel roofs and sides of the trucks, making the interior like ovens. We had to sit there hour after hour, naked except for a loin cloth or a pair of shorts, the perspiration pouring off us.'

13 was the number of freight trains used to carry the **3,666** Australians and **3,334** British prisoners of 'F' Force from Singapore to Thailand. Each train carried around **500** to **600** men. To transport 'H' Force, the train party consisted of **22** steel trucks with **27** men in each one. An NCO or an officer was in charge in each truck. In addition, there was a truck carrying Lieutenant Colonel Oakes and two other officers of field rank, Captain Butler the force's adjutant, Lieutenant Austin the interpreter, and the Japanese guard.

300 kilometres was approximately how far the men of 'F' Force had to march through the jungle from Ban Pong railhead to reach their work camps, the longest distance any of the POW groups

The prisoners on their way to Thailand. (*AWM 157866*)

had to walk. The march lasted for about **2.5** weeks, which was covered in **15** stages of about **20** kilometres each. Marching was invariably done by night, between 20.00 hours and 08.00 hours.

Except for the first **2** stages the road was merely a rough jungle track. Falls, resulting in sprains and even broken legs, were frequent. Some **20** men went missing on the march, possibly having fallen into the hands of Thais armed with knives who hung on the tail of the column ready to strip off the equipment of any man who fell behind.[17]

RASC Adjutant Richard Laird was on that march: 'We were on unmade-up track and in the dark it was impossible to avoid the roughness of the track, which resulted in many cuts and bruises which later developed into tropical ulcers. Some nights it was so dark that we resorted to tying a piece of white cloth or towel onto our packs so that the man behind could have something to follow. We normally started our march at dusk and would arrive soon after daylight at the next staging camp (bivouac). All too often we were kept on parade all morning, sometimes up to twelve noon and frequently in full sun, to allow stragglers to catch up and for the Nips to get their figures right. At the end of that we had no more than a few hours before we were due to

Green Battalion of 'A' Force marching from Thanbyuzayat to its first camp, Kandaw, or 4 Kilo camp. (*AWM P00406.006*)

move out again in the evening, and during this time we had to get what food we could.'[18]

'No man was permitted to fall out,' reported Major John Parsons of the 2nd Battalion, Garhwal Rifles. 'Men who collapsed on the track were beaten with rifle butts or kicked until they crawled on.'[19]

Stanley Wood-Higgs summed up the feelings of the men of 'F' Force: 'It is difficult to convey the utter despair and despondency which pervaded our spirits on this inhuman march. Only our hatred of our captors, our fatalistic acceptance of every hardship saved us from just giving up physically and mentally.'[20]

1 in 1

was the gradient of the rocky precipice the POWs of 'C' work battalion had to clamber down to reach the site of their work camp at Tonchan which was on a ledge perched 300 yards above the Khwae Noi. Very often when the prisoners arrived at a camp site there was little or nothing prepared for them and that was the case at Tonchan. When the prisoners arrived there, they found just **2** huts, one which had been built but was a mere shell and the other had only half a roof. When the prisoners first arrived at Wampo there was no accommodation at all. The men simply had to lie down wherever they could find some shelter from the weather and roll up their blankets or whatever they had over their heads to protect them from the swarms of mosquitos.

The first job the prisoners had to undertake, therefore, was to build accommodation for themselves, as Hugh Clarke, one of a batch of **600** men of 'F' Force which arrived at Konyu 3 camp on 25 April 1943, recalled. The party 'halted in a small clearing in the jungle-covered plateau and were informed that this was our new camp – when we built it'.[21]

In some instances, the prisoners took over sites previously occupied by *rŏmusha* which had been left in a filthy and very unhygienic condition, the first job in such circumstances being to clean the site.

498 was how many men of the British Sumatra Battalion were captured and sent to work on the railway. These were the only British prisoners who worked on the Burma side of the railway. Of these, **140** did not survive.

534 is how many men of the 2nd Battalion, 131st Field Artillery, 36th Infantry Division (Texas National Guard) of the US Army, were sent to work on the railway after having been taken prisoner when the Dutch East Indies surrendered to the Japanese. Of these **86** or **16** per cent died in captivity.

323 This is the number of sailors who were sent to work on the railway from the cruiser HMAS *Perth*, which was sunk at the Battle of Sunda Strait. Of the **681** men in *Perth*'s ship's company the night she was lost, only **328** of them survived the battle, reaching the island of Java, of whom **5** died after reaching shore. The remainder were taken prisoner and were placed under Lieutenant Colonel John Wiliams of 2/2nd Pioneer Battalion AIF, making up 'Williams Force' of **884** men. Williams Force arrived at Thanbyuzayat in October 1942 and were moved to Tanyin, 35 Kilo Camp to start work. Of the *Perth*'s crew, **106** died on the railway.

There is also a claim that *Perth*'s cat called 'Red Lead' survived the sinking and was carried by his shipmates to the railway. According to author Rowland Perry, the cat survived attacks by a cobra, a tiger and Japanese soldiers before being finally left with a Thai family, dying of old age in 1965. There is no corroborating evidence to this, though the story has been widely accepted as fact.[22]

61,806 was the total number of POWs employed on the construction of the railway:

Area from	*Sent to*	*Total*	*British*	*Australian*	*USA*	*Netherlands*
Malaya	Thailand	**30,305**	**28,931**	**8,507**	**494**	**12,378**
FIC	Thailand	**700**	**700**			
Malaya	Burma	**7,201**		**4,497**	**192**	**2,512**
Sumatra & Java	Burma	**3,600**	**500**			**3,100**
Totals		**41,806**	**30,131**	**13,004**	**686**	**17,990**

1 dollar a day, is what natives from the countries occupied by the Japanese were offered if they volunteered to work on the construction of the railway – plus all the rice they could eat! They were also permitted to take their family with them if they wished for which they would get a further **50** cents allowance. These were not the same as the conscripted Burmese of 1942 referred to above, though usually they were treated in the same appalling way by the Japanese. Any of these workers who fell ill and were unable to work had **30** or **40** per cent of their pay retained by the Japanese paymaster. They were told this money would be paid to them at the termination of their contracts. Of course, the Japanese had no intention of keeping this promise, pocketing the money themselves. The Japanese also made them pay for any medicines they were given and they even charged to allow them to open gambling places. Most of the money the native workers were supposed to have ended up in the pockets of the Japanese one way or another.[23]

Between March 1943 and March 1944 a further intake of workers was required and approximately **75,000** paid labourers were recruited from Malaya, mostly Malays and Tamils. In addition, about **7,500** Javanese and **5,000** Chinese from Thailand were taken to help with the maintenance of the railway in the early part of 1944.

The rates of pay for these workers were as follows:

A daily wage for an earth worker – **3** baht
A daily wage for a leader of a group of **25** labourers – **4** baht
A daily wage for a leader of a group of **100** labourers – **5** baht
A daily wage for a leader of a group of **500** labourers – **8** baht

They were also promised that if it rained the workers would receive an additional 1 baht per day.

The Thai Labour Service also conscripted **166,000** civilians. Of these, around **74,000** deserted en route to the line and a further **13,200** deserted soon after they arrived at the railway camps. Their pay was **1** rupee and **4** paisa a day. They were promised they would only have to serve for **3** months.[24]

These figures are, however, unreliable, as Commander Ishida of the Railway Corps explained: 'The labourers were recruited mainly from Thailand, Malaya and Burma. They received a departing allowance and travel expenses in advance through their group leaders when signing their contracts. However, almost all Thais and not a few Burmese deserted and re-applied for the same job twice or three times to receive allowances again.'[25]

In total, **85,738** Burmese labourers were recruited – or more accurately conscripted – for the railway construction. The manner in which these men were acquired was, in itself later considered a crime, one perpetrated by the Burmese themselves. The central government had imposed a system which gave the whole power of recruitment to the local area's administration. The Japanese labour officers fixed the number of labourers required from the area and the local authorities would select the individuals. This led to widespread corruption, or what has been called 'a colossal racket'. The person compiling the list of those to be conscripted would select his enemies, or political opponents. He would put many more names down on the list than the Japanese had asked for and would make sure it included wealthy individuals who would be 'squeezed' to pay handsome bribes to have their names removed from the list. If, after those who could afford to bribe the official were removed from the list, there was not enough to meet the Japanese requirement, vagrants would be rounded up, given a small payment, and sent off with secret instructions to take the first chance to run away before reaching the construction camp. It has been estimated that around three-quarters of the conscripts did not arrive at their respective camps.

12

Yen a day was the 'travel allowance' for prisoner-of-war general officers which was to take effect on or after 1 April 1944. This was broken down into an allowance of **1.10** Yen for breakfast, **1.90** for luncheon, **3.00** for dinner and **6.00** Yen for lodging. Officers of field rank were granted **0.90**, **1.60**, **2.50**, and **5.00** respectively. For Company officers, probably meaning captains and first lieutenants, the rates were **0.07**, **1.30**, **2.00** and **4.00**. 'Sub-officers and Cadets' were allowed **0.50**, **1.50**, and **3.00** for lodging. NCOs were granted **0.40**, **0.60**, **1.00**, and **2.00**. The poor privates were only allowed **0.30** Yen for breakfast, **0.50** for lunch, **0.70** for dinner and **1.50** for lodging.[26]

Chapter 2

The Work Begins

0

On 5 June 1942, the Japanese survey unit erected a **0.0**-kilometre post at Nong Pladuk station, Thailand. Work on the railway began later that month, with orders for the railway to be completed by the end of 1943.

30–50

was the average size of the POW work parties. The railway workers were organised by the Japanese into Groups or Branches; some branches had as few as **2,000** workers, others as many as **12,000**. Two prisoner of war groups – Nos. 3 and 5 – operated on the Thanbyuzayat side of the railway; four –1, 2, 4 and 6 – worked forward from Ban Pong in Thailand.

The POW groups were divided into battalions which ranged from **600** to **1,000** men. The number of battalions posted to each

POWs collecting the rails for transporting out to the track, each of which weighed 96 pounds per foot. (*AWM P00406.039*)

camp depended on the size of the task to be undertaken. A camp could, therefore, hold as few as half a battalion or as many as five or six battalions. The **30–50** strong POW work parties, or *kumis*, were generally under the command of one of their own junior officers (a *kumicho*) who were responsible for making sure the allocated work was completed, though, sometimes, the prisoners were left at the mercy of the Japanese railway engineers with no officers to help protect them from the unfettered abuses many repeatedly suffered. Often, even when an officer was present, there was little he could do to stop the ill-treatment of his men, and he was likely to be beaten for attempting to intercede on their behalf.

Two such *kumis* would make a *han* under a section commander who would be a captain or above, who would be known as a *hancho*.

In all the camps the Japanese engineers demanded the maximum number of prisoners for work details. That number was determined by the following sum:

A = total camp strength, other ranks
B = number of hospital patients, hospital staff plus those required for camp duties
A – B = figure demanded for outside work

Before the onset of the 'speedo' period the Japanese were quite lenient in allowing a full complement of prisoners to remain in camp. At Konyu No.3, for example, in March 1943, those remaining in camp, in addition to those required to build the huts, were as follows:

Cooks = **30**; wood and water carriers = **20**; warrant officers and clerks = **10**; medical orderlies = **15**; camp police = **5**; batman = **3**; anti-malaria duties = **5**; an orderly for the Imperial Japanese Army (IJA) HQ = **1**; barbers = **2**.[1]

49,776

Official Japanese figures show that in April 1943, before the arrival of 'F' and 'H' Forces, **49,776** POWs were in the railway camps. By that time **628** men had already died.[2] This made a total of **50,404** that had been engaged on the railway up to that time.

This was before the start of the monsoon and the terrible period of the 'speedo'. Over the months the battalions became much reduced in size. In December 1943 one battalion numbered less than double figures and another one had just **12** of its original members. As a result, in March 1944 the battalion formations were scrapped.[3]

Depending on the size of the camp, the Japanese camp commanders were subalterns, warrant officers, NCOs, or even privates. In some instances, sergeants or sergeant majors were responsible for camps with as many as **2,000** POWs and there were Koreans (who were not permitted to hold any rank) who were in charge of camps holding several hundred prisoners.

Generally speaking, the camps were run by the Japanese Imperial Army's Prisoner of War Administration. Apart from a few short-lived sub-camps, the railway engineers took no part in the administration of the camps. However, the railway engineers usually outranked the Japanese camp commanders which meant the latter had to comply with whatever demands the engineers imposed.

1,026 was the strength of the first party of Australian POWs under Major Charles Edward Green which was the first to begin work on the Burma end of the railway. What became known as Green Force was split into two detachments for its move to the first work camp at Kandaw which was located **4** kilometres from the railway's terminus at Thanbyuzayat. The camp had been built by the Japanese 5th Railway Regiment and was filthy and infested with vermin, having previously housed Burmese workers. The camp was situated in a rubber plantation and was always damp and messy. In a report to the War Crimes Trials, Major Green submitted the following regarding 4 Kilo camp: 'The only latrines were those used by the natives. They were in a small gully, and were filled with water 6 inches of [i.e., from] the top and the whole area was covered in maggots. There was no kitchen at all and no hospital accommodation whatever. Immediate efforts were made to put the camp in order. Kitchens and latrines were built and an effort [was made] to improve the huts.'[4] In the Burma sector the work consisted chiefly of clearing dense undergrowth, felling great trees and making embankments and cuttings.

1

cubic metre of earth per man was how much the workers had to shift each day in building embankments near Wang Lan using picks and shovels made from metal gasoline barrels. This quantity was typical of the requirements along the line, though later this was increased. This was 'no great effort' Hillary Custance Green conceded for a man with a shovel, but the earth had to be loaded and carried to the building site. For this, **3** other men were required, making a team of **4**. As each man was expected to shift **1** cubic metre, this meant a total of **4** cubic metres had to be dug and moved.[5] Because of the lack of anything but the crudest of equipment, the only means by which they could shift the earth was in a rice sack slung between **2** poles.

Private Francis 'Snowy' Stevens described what happened one day when he was carrying stones in this manner with his friend Dave Tate: 'The Japanese in charge at the time was not satisfied with the number of stones, which we had placed on the bag; he threw more stones on top of our load, then, still not satisfied, sadistically, sat himself on the stretcher and made us carry him and all the stones over to the embankment, a distance of some hundreds of yards.'[6]

6

At Hintok groups of **6** Australians were set the task of digging earth and carrying it in stretchers to the top of a high embankment. On arrival the Japanese engineers marked out a plot of ground **6** feet by **3** feet to be dug to a depth of **6** feet and indicated that only when it was finished the prisoners could go back to camp.

1/3

At one point at Chungkai before the start of the 'speedo' period, the work was arranged on a contractual basis in that the men would commit to digging **1.1** metres a day. It was said that this represented just **1/3rd** of the work expected from the troops in a Japanese railway unit. The prisoners were given Sunday as a rest day, with some of the men working late on Saturday evening to ensure the contracted work was completed.[7]

In one period at Takanun, officers supervising the work of their men were required to act as 'tally clerks' for the number of baskets of spoil carried by the prisoners. After a short while the Japanese suspected that the officers were falsifying the figures,

Chungkai Cutting, **60** kilometres from the start of the railway at Nong Pladuk, was cut by British prisoners based in a nearby camp which later became a POW base hospital. This section of the railway is still in use and the cutting has been widened to accommodate the modern gauge trains.

and they were taken off that role, and at one stage the Korean guards themselves falsified the figures so that they could return to camp earlier.

The more experienced and competent Japanese engineers were employed on the more technically complex tasks, such as bridge building, leaving the less able with the simpler jobs, such as the building of embankments. Some of these found it difficult even to calculate a task, and if, for example, a task required the moving of **15** cubic metres of soil, that amount had to be taken from a rectangular hole **3** x **5** metres, and **1** metre deep, and no other shape was allowed. There were numerous recorded incidences where miscalculations were made by the engineers resulting in work having to be corrected or re-done altogether.

The lack of equipment also created extreme inefficiencies and severely limited the speed at which the railway was built. In deep cuttings it was not uncommon to see a chain of **20** men passing baskets of earth behind just **2** men with digging tools.

A typical working day began with reveille and breakfast in darkness at 06.00–07.00 hours. (All times were Tokyo times which are **2.5** hours ahead.) Parade for work was at first light

Original rails and sleepers on display at Hellfire Pass.

when the number of fit men were counted. If this was regarded as insufficient, the daily battle began between the Japanese and the POW officers, often resulting in the officers being beaten by the Japanese for daring to try and save the seriously ill prisoners from being forced out to work.

Major Cyril Wild wrote about what he called this grim daily spectacle which was repeated at the camps along the line: 'Emerging from their crowded huts or leaky shelters in the pouring rain, even the fitter men appeared gaunt and starving, clad in rags or merely loincloths, most of them bootless and with cut and swollen feet. In addition, some **50** or **60** sick men from "hospital", leaning on sticks or squatting in the mud, would be paraded to complete the quota ...Sometimes all of these, sometimes only a part, would leave the camp hobbling on sticks or half carried by their comrades.'[8]

Further inefficiencies were the result of some of the camps being situated a long distance from the railway. In the area around Hintok and Hellfire Pass, which was extremely rocky, with large embankments and deep cuttings, some of the working camps were so sited that workers had to march over rough hills some **6** to **7** miles a day. This meant the men left for work in the dark and returned in the dark, as much as **16** hours later.

At Songkurai No.2 camp in August 1943, the principal task was the building of a wooden bridge, about **100** feet long over a nearby river, and the prisoners were required to carry logs up to **20** feet long and over **1** foot in diameter for distances of **800** feet through mud up to their knees, while being constantly beaten.

Though most of the wooden bridges have long since disappeared, some of their foundations can still be found.

Nevertheless, the prisoners made the best they could of the situation they had been handed, as one officer saw as he transited through Hintok Road Camp: 'The latrines were made of wood, were clean and sixteen feet deep; they had made a complete water system out of hollow bamboo pipes and had rigged up showers in a bath place entirely carpentered from bamboo; and they had a silver bugle blown by a first-rate bugler, who made the calls sound more beautiful with the mountain echoes than I'd ever believed a bugle could sound.'[9]

In December 1943, the Japanese indicated that, in contravention of the Hague Convention, they would make POW officers work. This was not enforced at

Another cutting, this one at Hintok to the north of Hellfire Pass.

One of a number of ore skips which ran along light, narrow gauge tracks used for shifting rock and ballast on display at Hellfire Pass. Most of the rock was moved using cane baskets and rice sacks slung between bamboo poles.

all the camps. In some camps, however, the Japanese had made the officers work much earlier than this date.

In Wun Lun camp the Japanese insisted that officers made up the required numbers for the working parties which had been reduced through sickness and ill-treatment. The officers, under Lieutenant Colonel Swinton, flatly refused. That was until a truck was driven up with a machine gun mounted on the rear which was trained on the dissenting officers, who, of course, relented. There were similar scenes in many camps.

The officers, being unused to heavy manual labour, were, in many cases, less efficient than the other ranks and beatings by the Japanese with pick handles or even iron bars was a daily occurrence. Often, the Japanese took great delight in giving officers the worst or dirtiest jobs and took equal pleasure at beating officers in front of their own men.

200

is how many officers volunteered to help improve living conditions at Ban Pong camp. Towards the end of October 1942, it was evident that a hospital was urgently required to accommodate the growing number of sick prisoners, and Lieutenant Colonel Williamson asked for volunteers from among the younger, more able, officers to be involved in the construction work. Scores of officers stepped forward to work alongside skilled native carpenters to build **2** huts, each of which could hold **240** patients.

These officers also saw that mosquito larvae were breeding in a pond to the north-east of the camp. It was the volunteer officers again, some **200** of them, who drained the pond, digging a drain **1,300** metres long.[10]

256

Naturally, when Major General Shimoda, who was the Japanese officer in charge of the building of the railway, was shown what the officers had done, he asked Colonel Williamson if the officers would like to volunteer to work on the railway itself. Remarkably, **256** officers actually offered to work, providing they were given work befitting their rank and that they were supervised only by Japanese commissioned officers. This was agreed and, from January 1943, the officer section began building small bridges over the many streams and ravines which the rail line had to cross.[11]

300

metres is the length of the famous bridge at Kanchanaburi over the Mae Klong River, with **11** spans of **20.8** metres carried on

Bridge building in progress. Though the location of the bridge is not indicated, the curved steel sections being lifted are similar to those on the bridge over the Mae Klong at Kanchanaburi. (*AWM 119182*)

well curbs and cement concrete piers, **20** metres above the river. The main part of the bridge came from Java where it was dismantled and shipped to Thailand in sections. This took **16** months to complete, from February to June 1943. When the prisoners arrived, they were told they had to build two bridges over a stretch of the river that was then known as part of the Mae Klong River. These, it is usually presumed, were the bases of the famous book and film *The Bridge on the River Kwai*. The first of these at Tamarkan, would be a temporary structure of wood to carry construction vehicles and supplies across the river while a more substantial concrete and steel bridge was being erected. In addition, they would also have to build around **2** kilometres of embankment on either side of the main bridge.

Unlike the character in Pierre Boulle's novel, Colonel Nicholson, the senior British officer in charge of the prisoners, Lieutenant Colonel Philip Toosey, did not cooperate with the Japanese to help expedite the building of the bridge. He stood up for his men and stood up to the Japanese commander. What he did do was take control of organising the work parties away from the Japanese, handing that responsibility to the POW

Bridge building was considered by some of the prisoners to be interesting work requiring skill and thought compared with the mundane tasks of digging, lifting and carrying which was what so many were forced to do.

officers, thus reducing friction between the prisoners and the Japanese or Korean guards. The Japanese engineers were persuaded to provide a list of men they would require each evening for the following day. That way, the officers were able to organise the men efficiently, saving a great deal of unnecessary confusion and arguing, and lessened the strain on the men. This increased efficiency may have helped the Japanese a little, but it was not the principal reason for the measure Toosey employed.

Toosey also managed to persuade the Japanese camp commander, Lieutenant Kosakata, and the Japanese railway engineers that they would get their bridge built far quicker if the men received better treatment. The result was that rations were increased, the working day was from 09.00 to 18.30 hours with a one-and-a-half to two-hour break in the middle of the day, and the men got one day's rest – a *yasume* – at least every **10** days.

This paid almost immediate dividends for both sides with sickness rates dropping rapidly. and more work being accomplished on the bridge. This in no way meant the prisoners worked willingly in the construction of the bridge, as is portrayed in the famous film. As Captain Ernest Gordon made clear, 'We

Just one of 680 trestle bridges built along the railway. This one was built near Songkurai camp. (*AWM P00406.002*)

worked at bayonet point and under the bamboo lash, taking any risk to sabotage the operation whenever the opportunity arose.'[12]

Toosey was in command of Tamarkan camp from October 1942 until December 1943. The camp was built in that October by a party of **200** all ranks under the command of Major Roberts of the 80th Anti-Tank Regiment. They were joined by **110** men of the Argyll and Sutherland Highlanders in March 1943. Their arrival was replicated in one of the most famous scenes in the film *The Bridge on the River Kwai.* It was recorded by Probationary Officer Masaru Tsuruta of the 6th Company, 3rd Battalion, 9th Japanese Railway Regiment: 'I heard the faint whistling of a march tune far away, at the other side of the palm forest. The whistling gradually came closer to us with the sound of the army boots of a big group. The tune they were whistling was the "Colonel Bogey March."'[13]

Toosey also agreed with the Japanese for his officers to engage in work on the bridge and the railway, even though this was in contravention of the Geneva Convention of 1929 which stated that, 'Belligerents may employ as workmen prisoners of war who are physically fit, other than officers.' This agreement that his officers could undertake manual labour came about because Toosey insisted that officers accompanied the work parties to try and mitigate the worst offences committed by the Japanese. The Japanese railway engineers watched the officers standing around and saw a potential additional resource and demanded that the officers worked as well. This was sparked by an incident when a Lieutenant Black was ordered to work instead of merely supervising his men. Black refused and was taken and placed under arrest in the camp's guard house.

This brought matters to a head, with the Japanese camp commander demanding that all officers must work. Toosey called a meeting at which he said that officers would still be able to protect their men and that they should agree to work, however, that the decision was up to individuals, and he would not order officers to work and 'If you refuse, I will stand and get shot with you'.[14] The meeting ended with a unanimous decision to work with their men. Over time, however, the officers resumed their previous supervisory role without any objection from the Japanese.

1/14th

This is what Lance Corporal Ian Dennys Peek calculated one of the Japanese engineers, Hasegawa, considered the prisoners to be equivalent to an elephant. There were around **50** elephants employed daily on the railway and **2,000** bullock carts.[15] When an elephant refused to carry a load because it considered the weight to be too great, Hasegawa would call for **7** pairs (i.e. **14** men) of POWs to perform the task in question.

The way this was done, was each pair would pick up a bamboo pole and a rope sling. The slings would be laid on the ground and the log levered onto the slings. The POWs would then pass the poles through the end loop of the sling. The men would bend their knees, put their shoulders under the bamboo and together, in one movement, straighten up. The prisoners would then carry the long to the required location.[16]

By contrast, when the elephants could be persuaded to move the logs, the procedure was quite simple. Each elephant would drag the logs along with chains while one POW would follow behind. When the allotted place had been reached the prisoner would undo the chains. The elephant would then kneel down and roll the logs into place.

During the height of the rushed construction of the 'speedo' period, some **200** elephants were employed along the line. One day, an additional load was added to one of the elephants above the usual two logs that the animals were expected to pull. The elephant refused to move. A guard deployed the normal Japanese method for solving problems by hitting the elephant between the eyes with a heavy tool: 'The elephant roared and started on him,' remembered one of the watching prisoners. 'The guard turned and ran for his life. The elephant chased him, teak log and all in tow, as he crashed along at full pelt. Even with the load, the elephant gained on the guard, so he ran down the embankment towards the river. The elephant followed and down they both went – the elephant sliding down on his bottom like in a Walt Disney picture! They crashed into the river below and the elephant set about squirting water at him through his trunk. The terrified guard swam to the other side to get away.' A few days later when the guard was on duty, the elephant recognised him and charged after him again. Eventually the guard had to be transferred.[17]

A similar incident happened at Songkurai camp to an elephant the prisoners had named 'Elphie'. This was described by Lionel de Rosario: 'One day Elphie was struggling to shift her load. A visiting Japanese officer believed he could deal with the situation in the usual manner – by giving her a bash on the head with her driver's prodding iron. Elphie was enraged and tried to charge her assailant but was held back by her chains and the weight of her load.'

A few weeks later, the Japanese officer returned to Songkurai and was recognised by Elphie. This time her load was not too heavy and, with a fierce trumpet call, she charged after the officer, dragging her load behind her. The officer ran for his life with Elphie in hot pursuit. As it happened, Elphie's logs became entangled in a tree which brought the elephant to a halt and her quarry escaped. It was the last time the officer was seen at Songkurai.

Elephants were also used to carry containers of water for the teams working on Hellfire Pass. Their Burmese drivers soon contracted cholera, however, and died. The Japanese tried to take command of the elephants, but the great beasts refused to cooperate. When one Japanese tried beating an elephant to make it obey, it picked the man up with his trunk and hit him against a tree.[18]

60

This was the weight in pounds of the rails per metre length of those used in the southern, Thailand, side of the railway, which came in **30**-foot lengths. Some of the Burmese rails were also **60** pounds per metre though others weighed **75** pounds per metre, with lengths of either **30** feet or **39** feet.

The sleepers were cut from hardwood trees and measured **10** inches by **6** in section. Ballast was to be created from broken stone found locally and from river-bed gravel.[19]

The process of laying these in place was as follows: Firstly, the ballast would be laid to depths of between **1** and **5** feet depending on the nature of the ground. The rails and sleepers were moved up to where the track was being laid by 'sleeper-carriers' and 'line-carriers' on **2** four-wheeled bogies. On the floor of the bogies were runners. Ten lengths of rail were strapped

Prisoners laying sleepers on the bed of the track. (*AWM P00406.028*)

to the bogies which were moved to the very edge of the last rail laid and its handbrake firmly applied. A tripod was then placed either side of the bogies. The prisoners would push the lengths of track along the bogies' runners onto runners on the tripods. When the lengths were clear of the bogies, a handle would be pulled which released the lengths from the tripods onto the ground. One gang would then shoulder the sleepers and place them on the prepared track at even spaces while the laying team would lever the lengths of track with crowbars.[20] The rails were attached directly to the sleepers by spikes by the spike team, with **4** spikes to each sleeper.

As the day progressed fatigue began to tell, and the blows of the hammer men on the spike team were not always accurate and the spike was sometimes bent. 'If the Jap engineer saw the work stop for a minute for a bent spike to be straightened or pulled out,' recalled Roy Whitecross, 'he bounded along muttering or screaming abuse, and laid about him with his heavy metre stick.'[21]That metre stick was carried by the engineers to check the width of the track to ensure the gauge was maintained.

The process of hammering the spikes could be a dangerous one. Many of the sleepers were made of teak, the hardest and densest of woods. Frequently, the spike would penetrate about **1** inch and then fly out of the sleeper to inflict terrible lacerations of the spikers' legs. The wounds would immediately become infected, resulting in terrible tropical ulcers.[22]

300,000 cubic metres of rock was excavated in the construction of the railway and **4,000,000** cubic metres of earth was shifted. The most notable rock cutting was Konyu cutting which became known as 'Hellfire Pass'. This was in **2** sections: one about **500** yards long by about **25** feet deep and the other approximately **80** yards long and **80** feet deep.

The work was begun on the pass with approximately **400** Australians on ANZAC Day, 25 April 1943. At first, they had to clear away the earth with the daily task set at **1.5** metres a shift, but within two days it was increased to **2** metres; by the end of the week, it had been set at **3** metres, and the layer of earth having been removed, the prisoners were encountering solid rock. This meant that by June the work had slipped behind schedule and further Australian and British POWs were transferred to the pass taking the workforce up to around **1,300**. These men worked around the clock in **3** eight-hour shifts of **400** at a time. In addition, there were approximately **2,000** native workers, half of whom were at the site at any one time. There were also around **20** Japanese who worked on the pass, operating in **2** twelve-hour shifts.[23]

One of the 'taps' used to cut Hellfire Pass is still embedded in the rock face.

5 Just **5** drilling machines were provided for the job of cutting through the rock of the pass. The cuttings were made by the 'hammer and tap' method. One man would hold a spike sharpened – the tap – at one end against the rock face while his partner would hit the spike with an **8**-pound sledgehammer. They had to

Another cutting the prisoners had to make was at Arrowhill, 110 Kilo camp.

repeat this process with increasingly longer drills until the hole was **60** cm deep. Into the holes the Japanese engineers placed an explosive charge, as explained by Australian Hugh Clarke. 'The engineers would get six or seven of us out and give us a cigarette. We would light a cigarette each. With these we would have to light four or five fuses and then go for our lives up into the bush before the charges blew.'[24]

Often the weaken and exhausted men would miss the spike and hit the poor partner holding it causing severe injuries, as did the flying splinters of rock. Crude hand drills were also used which spat out rock dust which covered the sweating workers, with larger splinters flying everywhere causing many injuries. After the dynamite had blasted away the rock, the prisoners had to clear away the resultant spoil with shovels and bare hands, after breaking the rocks down to a manageable size with sledgehammers.

Initially, the two man hammer and tap teams were expected to drill **80** centimetres per day, but this quickly went up to **300** centimetres and the prisoners could not stop until they had drilled and cleared the stated amount.[25]

12–16 was the number of hours the men of 'H' Force were made to work each day on Hellfire Pass. After marching all the way from Bam Pong and due to the monsoon rain having to wade through mud, often waist-deep, in the latter stages of its march to Kanu, the prisoners were made to clear a jungle area and construct a camp. This was completed the following day, and then work began: 'Blasting and clearing, blasting and clearing, in frantic forced shifts, from that moment until the railway was completed, we were given no rest or quarter,' wrote Ronald Searle. 'Thrashings began immediately, and the deathroll set off ...hour after hour, day after day, thrashings and beating continued unmercifully, 12–16 hour shifts became the rule, a little food could be hurriedly eaten only when blasting began ...Throughout the months in scorching sun and, more often, in stabbing monsoon rain, we dug away blast spoil and dragged great rocks to the cliff edge, tearing our flesh, straining our bellies, huddling under our remaining rags to get what protection we could against the bitter night of the mountains ...Beatings continued with monotonous regularity. Scalps were split with blows from a shovel blade, heavy bamboo rods were a favourite weapon, as was the pick helve. Heads and shoulders were battered black and blue. A man collapsed with fatigue and rolled down the mountainside; one Jap ordered two truckloads of rocks to be tipped down onto him in an effort to bury him alive.

'Any sign of exhaustion or weakness would bring a "beating up". If a club wasn't handy then sharp flints would be used to gouge the prisoner's arms. Legs swollen with beriberi or eaten away with maggot infested ulcers would be kicked or struck. Japs would gather and laugh at this; it was their daily entertainment.'[26]

Hugh Clarke described working on Hellfire as being 'like a scene out of Dante's inferno. The Japs decided we would work twenty-four hours a day, two shifts, one was the day shift and one was the night ...If you stood on the top of the cutting you would see the burning fires at intervals of about twenty feet; you'd see the shadows of the Japanese with their Foreign Legion caps moving around with their sticks belting men. There was shouting and bellowing. And this went on all night.'[27]

8 was the number of POWs who died as a result of injuries sustained falling into the cutting. A total of **69** prisoners were beaten to death by Japanese guards. One of these incidents was recorded by Captain Jeffery English. A prisoner holding a 'tap' who had fingers on one hand broken when his mate accidentally hit him with his sledgehammer, was not allowed to leave the pass to have his fingers set. Instead, he was given the job of turning the big crank which worked one of the generators floodlighting the cutting. 'The handle was too heavy for him to turn with his one good hand, and every time he flagged and the lights dimmed he was beaten with a bamboo,' recalled English. 'He was kept at it for nearly an hour, during which time he twice fainted; but when he fainted for the third time he didn't come round.' The man was carried back to camp by his comrades at the end of the shift, and he died a week later.'[28] It has been estimated that the total number who died working on the pass may have been as many as **400**.

10 minutes break every hour was granted to the workers from Takanun in the excavation of a cutting. As elsewhere, the prisoners were divided into teams of **4**, with one man to pick the cutting face of the rock, one to shovel and two men to carry away the excavated material in the usual bamboo and sling stretchers. This last task meant having to carry shale, rock or soaking clay for a distance of **50** to **75** yards through yellow oozing clay on a bed of gravel. Needless to say, the men's feet were badly cut at the end of every day. The **10** minutes break was classed as a smoke break, but for those suffering from dysentery and diarrhoea those few minutes was their chance to relieve themselves.

20 It was common enough for a man with dysentery to have to pay **20** visits a day to the latrines. While working on the railway this meant a journey of a few yards into the jungle – for there were no latrines there – and, as S. Dawson observed, 'the Japanese took it upon themselves to limit these visits as much as possible. To dash into the jungle and be caught coming back without having asked permission was to qualify for a slapping. And if one did ask permission, it very often pleased the Nip to keep one standing at attention until it was too late.'[29]

130 In April 1943, the Japanese hit on a plan to get more out of the workers with an incentive scheme. They confiscated goods from

The laborious process of laying the steel rails. (*AWM P00406.017*)

the canteen and then a list was compiled of those men who had worked well each day who were called out at *tenko* in the evening and handed these items as a '*presento*'. Predictably, as Lieutenant Colonel E. E. 'Weary' Dunlop complained, it meant 'some silly asses' fell for this and shifted as much as **130** loads a day. This then became the standard which all the prisoners were expected to carry.[30]

17

is how many days it took to complete the incredible Wampo viaduct, but it involved the labour of around **2,000** men. The Khwae Noi makes a sudden eastwards loop into a rocky gorge near the village of Wampo and almost cuts into the line of the railway. In order to carry the railway round the gorge, a ledge had to be created. This was cut from the top of the rock face downwards.

The main work camp was on the opposite side of the river which the prisoners had to cross each day to work. This was during the dry season when the water level in the Khwae Noi was so low that the prisoners could wade most of the way across, only having to swim a short distance in the middle of the river.[31]

To form the ledge for the railway the rock had to be blasted away in the same fashion as the Hellfire pass was excavated. The splinters from the explosions could fly considerable distances and, on one occasion, a piece of rock hit one of the POW cooks in the camp across the river. It entered his skull, exposing his brain. He survived with no lasting effects, but another prisoner working on the viaduct was not so lucky. A large piece of rock struck him in the face which resulted in permanent disfigurement and partial facial paralysis.

300 was the number of diesel motor trucks sent by the Japanese Southern Army to help with transportation during construction of the railway. These operated on a road largely built by the prisoners which ran roughly adjacent to the railway. The road was completed on 5 April 1943, but on the Thai side, it was nothing more than an improvement of a pack-horse way with many curves, upon which the trucks ran at an average speed of about **10** kilometres per hour with an average maximum loading capacity of **1** ton (though the average was only about **500** kilogrammes).[32] On the Burma side, the road constructed parallel with the railway was comparatively well built. To help maintain these vehicles the Japanese motor repair corps was increased by the addition of **2** corps of **5** sections each.[33]

18–20 was how many hours out of every **24** that it rained during the monsoon in May and June 1943.[34] Because of the resultant rising of waters in the Khwae Noi, land traffic was superseded by water traffic, and by the end of July 1943 the water line of communications was completed between Ban Pong and Nikke (**270** kilometres). The Thai government was also asked to provide craft to help with the supply of goods and equipment up the river and by the end of July more than **700** tugboats and **1,200** lighters were secured.

90 That is the maximum number of men that could be accommodated in the **6** small tents which had been provided for Captain John Lawrence Hands when he arrived at Hintok with 'A' battalion of **337** men and approximately **600** Dutch troops. As the work progressed the prisoners were moved further along the line as required and in most cases no provision had been made for their arrival, the men having to clear an area of jungle before they could start building any form of accommodation. Captain Hands' experience was typical of this. Those for whom there was no space in a tent had to sleep outside on the ground. Usually, in such circumstances a rota system was introduced so that everyone had their turn at sleeping under cover.

1, 2, 3

In most cases, the wooden upright supports for the large number of bridges which had to be built to carry the railway over rivers and ravines were made from trees which were **12** inches thick and which were pile-driven into the riverbed.

The pile-driving process was done with a metal weight on a wooden frame. A rope and pully were attached to the weight, enabling the prisoners, often waist-deep in the water, to haul the weight to the top of the frame. On command, the workers would let go of the rope and the weight would hit the upright which would be driven into the riverbed. The process would be repeated until the Japanese engineers were satisfied the upright was sufficiently bedded in. The sound of the Japanese shouting '*Ichi, Ni, San*' ('**1**, **2**, **3**') through a loudspeaker could be heard echoing along the river, as the prisoners pulled the weights to the summit. Then on the command '*Yon*' ('**4**'), the rope would be released.

The prisoners would have to work in the river for hours performing this task with no respite. During the monsoon the Khwae Noi became fast-flowing and large items, including tree trunks carried by the rushing waters caused many accidents to the prisoners, some fatal, much to the amusement of the Japanese.

An extreme example of this was spotted by Lieutenant Colonel F.J. Dillon, the senior officer of 'F' Force. He found a party of **20** prisoners who had been on their way from Shimo-Nieke to Nieke camp when they were intercepted by Japanese engineers and put to work pile-driving in the Khwae Noi. They had been forced to work each day from first light to 22.00 hours up to their armpits in cold, swift running water the whole time except for half an hour for lunch and 'driven with blows and sticks'. By the time Dillon discovered them they were in a terrible state and only **3** were fit for any work at all. Dillon managed to rescue them, but the men were 'too far gone', and all of them died.[35]

Track laying in Burma. Many hands did not make light work for the PoWs. As can be seen, the rails were moved up to the laying point on bogies. (*AWM P00406.034*)

6 kilometres was how much track a Japanese railway platoon of **60** men would be expected to construct, using POW and native labour. Second Lieutenant Juji Taramuto's platoon of the 3rd Company, 9th Railway Regiment had to build this length of track between Matoma and Rin Tin camps. This included **6** wooden bridges of **30**, **10**, **40**, **120**, **12** and **12** metres in length.[36]

20,000 was how many cubic metres of earth would have to be shifted each day as well as the building of **10** metres of bridging when, in January 1943, Imperial General Headquarters demanded that the railway must be completed by August of that year. This rushed building work resulted in what became known as the 'speedo' period of construction.

Each day the workforce was divided into sections. Each section was given an identical task to complete, irrespective of the nature of the ground, some parts being easier to shift than others. Any protests at the inequality of this would result in a beating. The soil was carried by one person in a basket or by two men in makeshift stretchers.

120 degrees Fahrenheit (almost **50** degrees Celsius) was the temperature the men had to work in during the hot, dry season. This was noted by Private Haig Logan, who was a member of the ill-fated 'F' Force: 'Except for our G strings we worked naked and barefoot in heat which reached **120** degrees. Our bodies were stung by gnats and insects, our feet cut and bruised by sharp stones. Somewhere the guards had picked up the word "speedo". They stood over us with their nasty staves of bamboo yelling "Speedo. Speedo" until "speedo" rang in our ears and haunted our sleep. When we did not move fast enough to suit them, which was most of the time, they beat us.'[37]

A surviving spike with which rails were attached to sleepers.

50 The ratio of labourers employed on construction to the total strength in labour camps was said to be at best **50** per cent, those not employed on construction being either on camp duties or in hospital. Through the spring and summer of 1943 this condition is said to have deteriorated causing a further decrease in the ratio so that at the point of highest production and labour capacity (approximately **200,000**), frequently the number of labourers available daily for construction could not have been more than **50,000**.

24

is how many hours Private Eric Bertrand Hilton of the 5th Bedfordshire and Hertfordshire Regiment was made to crouch down, stripped naked, with his hands tied, being repeatedly bashed by Japanese and Korean guards. Hilton had been out on a working party when he stopped for a moment to urinate. A Korean guard, Carmada, saw this and gave Hilton a 'preliminary' beating – but instead of taking his punishment, Hilton struck back and hit the Korean.

Hilton was never going to be allowed to get away with this and he was handed over to a Japanese sergeant called Nakamura. The sergeant made Hilton stand outside the guard room for **24** hours, the guards intermittently assaulting him. A trial was then ordered, the tribunal consisting of the camp commander, Lieutenant Uzuki, along with Carmada and Nakamura. Hilton was not present at the trial but Captain A.W. Coxon, Adjutant of 1/5 Sherwood Foresters answered some questions on his behalf.

After the first sitting of the tribunal, Hilton then had to endure the punishment referred to above, being left in a crouching position for 24 hours. After the second sitting of the court a decision was reached. Gunner Stanley Taylor reported what happened next: 'At 2 p.m. the same day he was taken away by Lieut. Usuku, Sjt Nakamura, Korean Motoyama and Korean Yuki. I saw him being taken away and I noticed that they had with them some rifles, I drew my own conclusion as to what was going to happen. About an hour and a half later the same four men returned but without Hilton, and I was given the rifles to clean.'[38]

Beatings could be given for the mildest of offences. In one case, a Sergeant Jordan was found asleep in his hut by one of the Japanese guards. The guard, called Kanemura, woke Jordan up and told him to go outside. He took the prisoner a short distance away and asked him politely if he liked football. Jordan answered that he did. The guard then told Jordan to kneel down, and said to the prisoner, 'Then I'll play football with you,' and started kicking

Jordan 'everywhere'. All Jordan could do was protect his face with his hands allowing the guard to kick him all over his body. This lasted for about **15** minutes before the guard became tired and then he continued hitting the prisoner with his fists. Jordan was hospitalised for **3** months.

30 is how many prisoners from Tamuang camp who were in a working party shifting 'gravel' (probably ballast) in July 1944. Each prisoner was carrying **2** sacks suspended from a bamboo pole. One of the prisoners emptied his sacks in the wrong place, and the "Black Prince" [Kinzo Motoyama], who was one of the guards with us,' a witness later wrote, 'picked up a chunkle (a tool like a bent spade) and struck him a blow over the head with it. The prisoner staggered a few steps, and as he did so, the Black Prince kicked him on the legs and he dropped to the ground.' The prisoner died.[39]

In another incident, an unnamed prisoner of the Royal Artillery, got his foot caught under a road roller which crushed the toes and instep, and he was unable to continue working. For this Motoyama beat the man with a bamboo stick so severely he was hospitalised.[40] At the war crimes trials held after the war Motoyama was sentenced to death by hanging.

Chapter 3

Life in the Camps

6 is how many branches there were of the Thailand POW Administration. The majority of the work camps were run by the Administration entirely separately from the railway regiments. Organised on 15 August 1942 in order to house and feed the POWs, it became operational on 1 October of that year. Each of the **6** branches was composed of **7** officers, **17** non-commissioned officers and around **30** clerical military employees.

In theory, the Japanese engineers had no jurisdiction over the camps. In reality, the railway engineers usually outranked the camp guards who were often commanded by junior officers or NCOs who were, consequently, forced to obey the engineers. The camps of 'F' and 'H' Forces were controlled by the Malayan

The accommodation huts at Kanchanaburi. (*AWM P1502.008*)

POW Administration. As this body had no authority in Thailand, it always struggled to procure enough food.

45 were the number of articles of the Geneva Convention which the Japanese Government agreed to adhere to regarding the treatment of American prisoners of war on 24 February 1942, providing the same applied to Japanese prisoners held by the United States. In a letter agreeing to this and laying down in detail each of the articles, the Ministry of Foreign Affairs claimed that POWs would be treated even better than the convention's stipulations. They would not be forced to perform labour against their will; they would be provided with bread, butter, eggs, meat, heating oil, coal and fats. They would also be able to receive gifts of food and clothing. Internees would be visited regularly by a doctor and would be permitted to read books, newspapers and listen to Japanese radio. Of course, none of this happened with the American or any other POWs that were sent to work on the railway.[1]

4 was generally the maximum percentage of POWs permitted to remain in a camp to run the cookhouse. In some camps this was as low as **1** per cent. These men had to cut their own bamboo for the fires on which they cooked the food and boiled water to sterilise it, they also often had to carry their own water and carry all the rations from the railhead or riverside. As a result, casualties among them were high, for example at Tarsao, Tonchan and the Kanyu camps mortality rates were between **40** and **50** per cent.[2]

Similarly, the number of men in total allowed to run a camp when the prisoners were first transported to Thailand and Burma in 1942 was **20** to **30** per cent. During the 'speedo' period when the Japanese demanded that every possible person should be made available for work on the railway, this number dropped to as low as **4** per cent.

70 is all the prisoners who were permitted to remain in Hintok Road camp out of a force of about **1,000** prisoners, or **7** per cent. This figure broke down as follows: **29** cooks, **15** medical personnel

Prisoners queuing for their rice ration. (*AWM 128455*)

(including two doctors, majors A. A. Moon and E.L. Corlette), **11** clerks, **6** men for anti-malarial work and hygiene, **5** for water carrying duties, **1** bugler and **3** batmen for the Japanese.

3

The prisoners were not supposed to have direct contact with the local inhabitants, though this was not enforced consistently during the period of the construction and running of the railway nor was it mandated at every camp. Nevertheless, anyone found disobeying this ruling when it was in force faced severe punishments. Sergeant H. Jones of the Royal Signals recorded in his secret diary what happened to a Thai woman and her **3** children in November 1942 at Ban Pong when she was caught trying to give some fruit to the POWs. They were 'hung by their thumbs from a fence for an hour and then taken down and tied up in front of the Korean guard room for 2 days in the boiling heat without food or water'.[3]

900

Possessing a wireless was also strictly forbidden but a number of radio parts were smuggled out of Singapore and reconstructed in the camps. They were hidden in all sorts of places, possibly the most common being secreted in a false bottom to a water carrier. The water bottle would be cut in half and a false bottom soldered on.

Anyone found having any involvement with a radio faced terrible retribution. The most widely known example of this was vividly described in the book, and later the film, *The Railway Man* by Eric Lomax. When a radio was discovered by the Japanese at Kanchanaburi, five POWs, all officers, were punished.

They were forced to stand at attention for a day and then, one by one, they were beaten with pickaxe handles and kicked: 'I went down with a blow that shook every bone, and which released a sensation of scorching liquid pain which seared through my body,' Lomax wrote. 'Sudden blows struck me all over ...I could identify the periodic stamping of boots on the back of my head, crunching my face into the gravel; the crack of bones snapping; my teeth breaking ...Yet the worse pain came from the pounding on my pelvic bones and the base of my spine. I think they tried to smash my hips.'[4] A doctor waited to tend to the wounds of

Kandaw Camp, 4 kilometres from Thanbyuzayat where work first began at the Burma end of the railway. (*AWM P01910.008*)

the battered prisoners. As he waited, he counted the blows the **5** men had received. He counted **900**. Four more officers were deemed to have been involved with the secret radio and were similarly beaten, **2** of whom died.

15

This was how many dollars were deducted by the Japanese from the pay received by the British and Commonwealth officers for food, clothing, light and lodging throughout their time on the railway in the appalling conditions they forced the prisoners to live. The amount the officers received was between **40** and **50** dollars a month, depending on rank. For example, a lieutenant colonel received **220** dollars a month. Of this, he received just **45,** less the **15** dollars deductions for food and accommodation, leaving him with just **30** dollars. The rest of the money was credited to accounts opened in the officers' names in the Yokohama Specie Bank.[5] In each Group a POW officer was designated to be responsible for keeping records of the amounts saved and was agreed monthly with the Japanese.

The pay was given out in dollars or the local currency. Deductions also varied throughout the period of captivity, with, at times, heavier deductions being made from the pay of officers of field rank, i.e. major and above.

For a period in September 1943, with conditions in the camps being so bad – or as the Japanese referred to it as 'the decreased cost of living' – the amount deducted from officers' pay for board and lodging was reduced to **20** *rupees* a month. The scale of payment to officers when this took effect was:

	Gross	*Board & Lodging*	*Bank*	*Net*
Major	**170**	**20**	**120**	**30**
Captain	**122.50**	**20**	**2.50**	**30**
Lieutenant	**85**	**20**	**35**	**30**[6]

Though there was a degree of variation in some camps, the general rule was that **40** per cent of the money officers received was deducted to buy extra food for the hospitals. Combat Other Ranks who worked were paid, on average, **25** cents per day – one-fifth of that offered to native labourers. This was about enough to purchase **1** duck egg. NCOs received **30** cents a day and warrant officers **40** cents.

In practice rates of pay varied considerably at different periods and according to the type of work done. Those involved in specialist tasks in connection with the railway construction, such as drivers, carpenters, blacksmiths, engineers, and rail-layers, were paid slightly more, ranging from **55** to **75** cents per

The Huai Ro Khi River by Kami Songkurai camp in full flood during the monsoon. It is considered locally that the bridge built here was more likely to be the one which inspired Pierre Boulle's *The Bridge on the River Kwai.*

Prisoners transporting attap which formed the roofs of the accommodation huts in the camps. (*Australian War Memorial; P00406.013 & .014*)

day for warrant officers, between **45** and **65** cents for NCOs, and from **40** to **60** cents for privates.

The lowest paid were those working in base hospital camps as cooks and those on other, though essential, camp duties. Of these, warrant officers received **25** cents per day, NCOs **15** and privates just **10** cents.[7] Red Cross Other Ranks (i.e., non-combatants) received rates which varied from **10** to **20** dollars a month. The pay was often at least a month late.

There were periods when pay was reduced or stopped altogether. One such instance was in 1945 when news that Germany, Japan's ally, had surrendered.

Throughout the period of construction, no IJA funds were provided for those too sick to work, at least officially. Some Japanese camp commanders did allow hospital patients half rations. 'No work, no food', was the Japanese mantra. To mitigate the effects of this in many of the camps all the food was 'lumped together' by the prison cooks and shared equally among workers and patients.

Even though they gave up a large proportion of their pay, the officers were still far better off than their severely undernourished men who lived for many months on the verge of starvation.

At Changaraya camp near the Thai-Burmese border Sergeant Stan Arneil noted that the officers were 'all well, have neither ulcers nor itch and are well shod,' and they had 'sugar, four tins of fish, tins of milk and as much soap, tobacco and oil as they wanted'. That the officers kept so much for themselves when their men were struggling to stay alive was, Arneil wrote, 'a wicked thing for the officers to do'.[8]

However, in February 1945, the net pay of officers who (apart from medical officers and padres) had by this time been separated from the Other Ranks and placed together in a camp in Kanchanaburi was reduced to a mere **20** ticals a month. This was because, the Japanese said, the officers had been spending their money on newspapers which was strictly forbidden.

Articles of clothing provided by the Japanese were not given to the prisoners, they were 'lent' to them. In reality, what little clothing was handed out to the POWs would be worn to shreds and would never be returned. In theory, the following was what the POWs 'may' be lent: **1** set of bedding, **1** field cap or summer cap, **1** suit of a summer blouse and pants, **1** suit of a summer vest and 'drawers', **1** suit of working clothes, 1 pair of socks, **1** pair of rubber-soled socks, and **1** pair of boots.

Strangely, there was supposed to be a monthly allowance granted to the POWs for the repair of clothing. Equally strange

POWs lining up for their morning ablutions. (*AWM P00761.006*)

is that officers, many, including officers of field rank, who did no work, were allowed **2** Yen for clothing repairs and the lower ranks, who were those most likely to need their clothes repaired, were allowed just **1.5** Yen.[9]

100

sheets of toilet paper was one of the 'Standard Scale of Necessities' which the prisoners were supposed to be given every month by the Japanese. Once a month they were also to receive **1** bag of tooth powder. Every **2** months they were to receive **1** towel, **1** cake of soap, **1** toothbrush and **1** loin cloth, and a pencil every **3** months. It was also stated that tobacco and/or other articles could be substituted for any of these items as long as the cost was the same.[10]

1

dollar is what a Private Bruce of the composite battalion of the Plymouth Argyle Royal Marines received as reward for jumping into the river to rescue a Japanese guard at Chungkai camp who had fallen into the river and was drowning. A parade was called by the Japanese commander who presented Bruce with an 'illuminated' testimonial, that **1** dollar, and was given the rest of the day off work.[11]

Members of 'F' Force, bathing and washing clothes on a washing platform in a stream at Kami Songkurai Camp No 3. (*AWM P02569.188*)

70

was the approximate weight in pounds of the largest recorded fish caught by a prisoner using improvised rod and line on the Khwae Noi. It was not uncommon for the Japanese and the POWs to work jointly to catch fish. The Japanese would throw grenades or sticks of dynamite upstream or from boats and the prisoners waiting downstream would collect the stunned or dead fish. The Japanese always took the greater share of the spoils.

50

was the weight in kilos of the bags of rice which had to be carried by the prisoners on their backs from the river or the railway to their respective camps. If any of the half-starved prisoners stumbled when carrying these enormous loads they were immediately beaten.

700

The standard Imperial Japanese Army scale of rations was **700** grams of rice per soldier per day. POWs were to receive **660** grams and the Asian workers **600** grams. This rice was of the poorest quality and the sacks were filled with floor sweepings and mixed with straw, rat droppings, weevils and maggots.

Basic rations were, in theory, requisitioned by the POWs twice a month – on the 1st and the 15th – from the nearest Japanese supply depot. They were distributed to the POW cookhouses by Japanese or Korean quartermasters who usually made money out of the prisoners by falsifying the quantities they issued. One trick was with bags of rice which were marked up on the outside as '**100** kilos'. It was easy for the quartermaster to change the number to read '**106** kilos' and then issuing it to the prisoners as the heavier weight. With no scales to check the weights it was impossible for the prisoners to disprove the number on the bag.

In addition to rice, all three of the above categories were supposed to receive **500** grams of vegetables, **5** grams of salt, **5** grams of tea, **5** grams of condiment and **20** grams of sugar. Dunlop Force, commanded by Colonel 'Weary' Dunlop, was divided into two battalions, each **450**-men strong: 'O' Battalion (commanded by Major H. G. Grenier) and 'P' Battalion (commanded by Major F. A. Woods). For the month of February 1943, 'O' and 'P' Battalions were entitled to **3,212** kilogrammes of meat and **18,000** kilogrammes of vegetables. They actually received

300 kilogrammes of meat and **4,500** kilogrammes of vegetables. The Japanese guards always took a greater proportion of these 'good commodities', it being estimated that **20** guards consumed as much as **100** prisoners.[12]

Even then, the rations were not evenly distributed, as Ernest Gordon wrote: 'To get our meals we formed a line in our huts. Our server would dip his can into the rice bucket and dump its contents into our mess tins. Another server would ladle out a watery stew of green leaves.

'I always watched warily when my turn came. I knew the servers would give me short measure so that they would have more for themselves and their chums. Yet I dare not protest or next mealtime I'd draw even shorter measure.'[13]

With Burma being the main rice-producing country in the region, the rice ration for POWs was, in general, met by the Japanese, but there were two problems associated with rice being the main source of sustenance. The first was that cooking rice was something new to most of the POW cooks and what they produced was unappealing: 'The only cooking utensil we had was a cast-iron pan called "quarlie",[14] about three feet wide and six inches deep. You make an earth support from this and burn the fuel underneath.' Explained Sergeant Frank Foster. 'Now I suppose most of you think that in countries so densely timbered as Burma and Siam there would be plenty of wood fuel. But there isn't. The rainfall is so heavy that all growing timber is green. The only fuel that is of any use is dead bamboo sticks, which we had to pull out from the middle of the prickly green clumps. This burns all right, in fact very fiercely for a few minutes; but then you have got to put on some more, and it's quite impossible to get that even heat which I now know is necessary for cooking rice. Then there was the problem of water. The only water we could get was from the muddy stream close by. As the fierce fire burned the rice in the bottom of the quarlie the amateur cooks added more muddy water. The result was a steamed and burnt brown lumpy dish of rice.'[15] It must be added that the rice given to the prisoners was off-white, containing broken reject grains, whereas the Japanese had 'beautiful white' rice. During the monsoon period, stored rice also became mildewed, and the

The site of Lin Tin or 181 Kilo Camp. This camp held predominantly Dutch prisoners. John Coast, who passed through the camp in May 1943, considered it to be 'the eeriest and foulest place we had seen in Thailand'. The hut is not a relic of the POW camp.

rice at the bottom of a sack often became hard with mould and age and had to be thrown away.[16]

Captain Wilson, RAMC, submitted a report on nutrition in the camps of 'F' Force, which read, in part: 'The Japanese QM would issue a certain number of bags or boxes of these commodities regardless of their state of fitness for human consumption and this total number would be shown on his records. The preserved meat, a coarse fibred meat, probably buffalo meat without bone, was partially salted or pickled and arrived packed in boxes. It usually swarmed with blowfly maggots and was usually in such an advanced state of decomposition that, as a grey-green fluid it dropped through the seams of the boxes. Only one box might be salvaged of meat worth cooking from four or five issued. Sacks of potatoes suffered greatly from wet during transit and storage, and many were only fit for the refuse pit.'[17]

Yet there were occasions when the prisoners were so hungry, even such meat was eaten. At Aungganaung camp several boxes of meat arrived in such a bad state that the Japanese commandant complained of the smell. 'The meat must be eaten forthwith,' he declared. The Australian commander replied that it was too bad to eat. The Japanese then ordered the meat to be buried since 'I cannot put up with the smell'. 'His house was 300 yards from where we were,' commented the Australian commander, 'and we had the meat!' Eventually much of the consignment was consumed by the prisoners.[18]

17 This was how many grubs one prisoner found in his rice in his midday meal and **14** in his evening meal. Apart from the poor quality of the badly prepared rice, finding it full of insects meant there were many instances of prisoners simply being unable to stomach the unappealing rice they were served up – certainly in the early stages until they became hardened to what they were offered.

This exacerbated the second problem, which was that the prisoners' digestive systems, used to a diet of bread, potato, pork and beef, could not assimilate the rice efficiently compared to the Asians for whom rice was their staple foodstuff. Having rice for every meal, especially rotten or mouldy rice, also led to the POWs experiencing digestive disorders which weakened them even further.

The 'polished', or white, rice the prisoners received lacked vitamin B1, a deficit of which led to prisoners developing beriberi, the effects of which are discussed in the following chapter.

1,200 calories per day is what the above-mentioned Captain Wilson calculated each person received at Nieke camp in June 1943. This was made up of **270** grams of white rice, **24** grams of dried lima beans and **50** grams of meat including bone. This is less than that required for basal metabolism. In other words, the prisoners were being starved to death.

'Time ceased to have any significance,' wrote Russell Braddon. 'No man knew what day of the week nor what week of the month nor even what month of the year it was ...If one were to survive it was essential not to acknowledge the horror that lay all around, still more not to perceive the effect it had upon oneself. It was not wise ever to look in a mirror. Life accordingly evolved into a blur of continuous work, people dying, guards bellowing, heavy loads to be carried, fever which came in tides of heat and cold on alternate days, dysentery and hunger. All those became the normal.'[19]

This is a photograph of Tamuang, or Tha Muang, which became one of the main camps for the prisoners after work on the railway had finished. The camp held around **12,000** Australian, British, Dutch and American prisoners.

45,000 is how many eggs were available for the prisoners at Konyu camp to purchase on 2 May 1943. These were provided by the Thai trader Boon Pong Sirivejjabhandu as part of his normal business, sanctioned by the Japanese, selling goods to the POW camp canteens. He also sold fish, sugar, oil, peanuts, onions, tobacco and soap. These eggs were duck eggs, which were larger than the Thai chicken eggs. Eggs were considered to be the most valuable supplement to the prisoners' basic rations which could be bought, and many men owed their survival to the ducks of Thailand.[20]

As well as this vital official business, Boon Pong became one of the heroes of the Thailand-Burma railway story. This dates back to September 1942, when Lance Corporal R.G. Payton of the Royal Army Service Corps on a ration collection trip from Ban Pong to Nong Pladuc, was handed a note which stated that civilian internees in Bangkok had heard disturbing reports about conditions in the POW camps in the interior. The note asked for more information. It was simply signed 'V', the widely recognised two-finger sign employed by Winston Churchill.

A reply was sent from the officer in charge of the RASC detachment at Ban Pong and Nong Pladuk, Major Sykes, describing conditions there as well as what was known about other camps brought down the line in secret notes by the RASC drivers. This was the start of a regular exchange of information and the monthly supply of small packets of medicines and money to the POWs.

The Hintok Tampi bridge located **90** kilometres south of Kinsayok. (*AWM 120507*)

The organisation was run by K. G. Gairdner who was one of around **200** British subjects interned by the Japanese in Bangkok. Gairdner's wife was a Thai lady who was able to move around freely. Over time, Gairdner sought to extend his organisation's reach to the camps further north that were served by Boon Pong.

14

Remarkably, we have records of some of deliveries of the items sent to the prisoners via Boon Pong who, unquestionably, risked his life helping the POWs. They were smuggled into the camp in various ways, such as hidden in bags of rice. We know, that on 5 June 1943 a consignment of **14** parcels was despatched and received on 26 June at Chunkai camp. The number of items is staggering, when it is considered that this was all done surreptitiously under the noses of the Japanese. The parcels included **42** hypodermic needles, **9** syringes, **6** surgical knives, **7½** lb of cotton wool, **96** bandages, **249** tablets of acetyl salicylic acid and literally hundreds of other pills such as aspirin, vitamin B, and quinoid to mention just a few. There were even anaesthetics in the form of **200** ampoules of morphine and **159** ampoules of novocaine.[21]

With regards to the supply of large quantities of eggs, it was not always the case that the POWs benefitted. On one occasion at

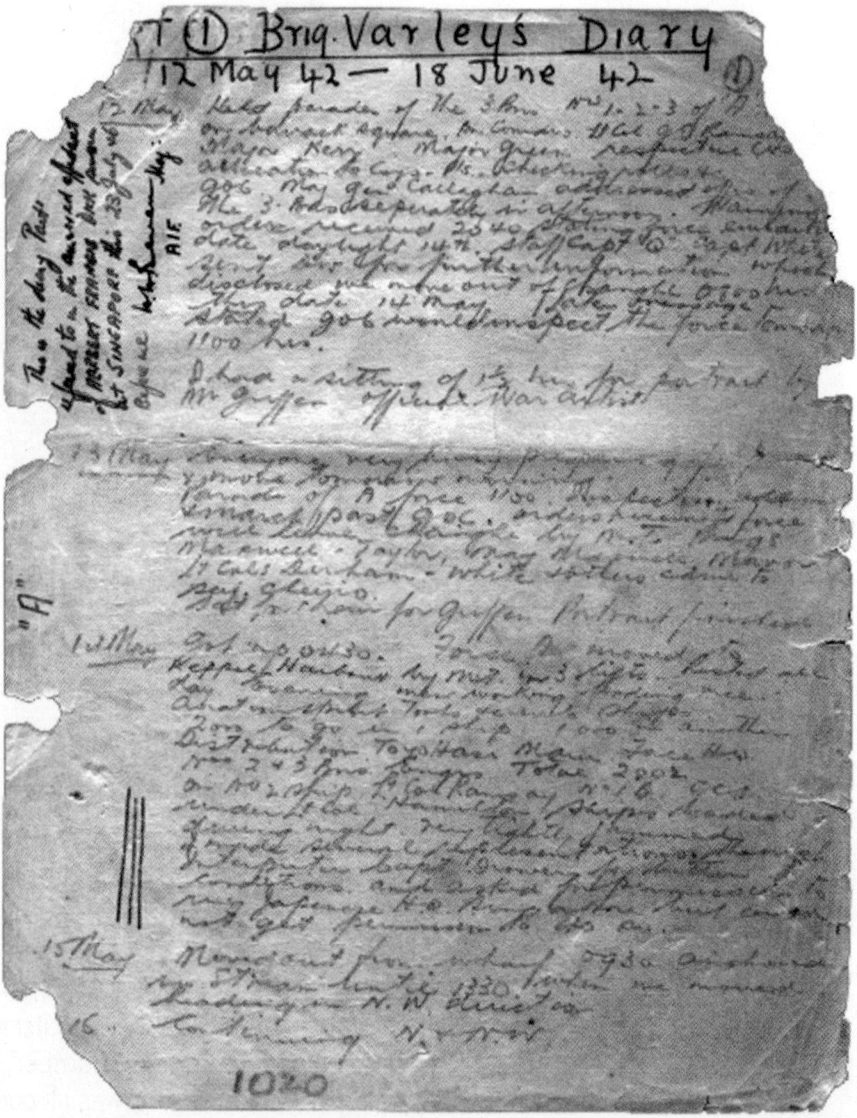
Brig. Varley's Diary
12 May 42 — 18 June 42
1020

The Japanese did all they could to prevent the prisoners keeping personal records of the true state of affairs in the camps and on the railway. Nevertheless, some courageous individuals took great risks to write down what they saw. Such was the case of the senior POW, Brigadier Varley, who kept a diary which had to be carefully concealed from the Japanese. (*AWM 2019.22.89*)

Hindaine camp **30,000** eggs were received. Of these **5,000** were given to the approximately **3,000** prisoners and the remaining **25,000** were kept by the approximately **75** Japanese. Another time **400** chickens arrived. Not one was given to the POWs.[22]

100

Meat on the hoof was provided from time to time in the form of native cattle, or yaks and there was one notable event when **100** of these beasts were driven to Krian Kri camp. A team of **19** prisoners under Lieutenant Geoffery Adams herded the yaks for **10** days through more than **120** kilometres of 'swamp, jungle mountain and stream' to bring this vital supplement to the meagre diet of the men. With just one Korean guard, Takeda, accompanying the prisoners, Adams' men considered killing him in the jungle and, with the cattle as food, escape to the hills. But the cattle they were driving meant an increased food supply for their comrades and a better chance of survival in camp than trying to escape.

After they had reached Krian Kri it became Adams' job to look after the herd and to slaughter one yak every second day. In this, the meat was divided according to a strict rule. One-quarter of the animal, plus liver and heart, went to the **23** guards and the remainder to the **900** prisoners.[23]

The Japanese claimed that over the course of the construction of the railway every few days cattle were herded up to the camps, and that 'almost **1,000** head of cattle were secured on the Thai side alone'.[24]

230

is the amount of rain in millimetres which falls in the month of September in Thailand at the height of the monsoon. The monsoon typically runs from May to October, the average rainfall per month is around **190** millimetres. Total annual rainfall in Thailand can be as high as **4,500** millimetres, with most of that falling during the monsoon. It is a similar picture in the southern regions of Burma/Myanmar with rainfall as heavy as **5,000** millimetres per year. Rainfall in the UK, by comparison, on average ranges between **800** millimetres to **1,400** millimetres.

The monsoon of 1943, which coincided with the 'speedo' period was the worst time of all for the POWs. 'We worked and lived in a world of wetness,' wrote Captain Ernest Gordon of his time at Chungkai camp: 'One day's labour was washed away by the floods of the next. Torrents strewed rocks in our path. We understood then how unfortunate was the location of our camp at the junction of the Kwai and the Mae Klong. Both rivers

The site of what used to be Kui Yae POW camp, then and now. This was an entirely Dutch camp until the arrival of **100** Australians of Major Cough of 'D' Force V Battalion at the end of August 1943.

overflowed and left us living on a raft of mud almost up to our sleeping platforms.'[25]

Lieutenant Colonel Roland 'Roly' Oates' party arrived at Malay Hamlet camp to work on Hellfire Pass in May 1943: 'Almost immediately the monsoon rains began, pouring down day after day, until the country became like a wet sponge. In our confined area, and on the track outside which carried the traffic, mud was often knee deep – filthy, oozing mud which stuck to everything like glue ...I doubt if any of us or our belongings were dry during the first month in that camp.'[26]

Max Offerle was one of the American prisoners at Anganan camp where a stream ran through two of the huts reaching a depth of up to **1** foot. The water was so deep the prisoners caught and ate lungfish that swam under the huts. He wrote the following about conditions at the camp during the monsoon period: 'Actually, creeks and rivers form, and you can almost watch vegetation grow. The rainy or monsoon season turned everything to soup or mud, and they couldn't get supplies up there easily ...Well, the men's health broke down. We started getting lots of malaria, beriberi, dysentery, and tropical ulcers because it seemed that the germ that causes tropical ulcers was more prevalent in the rainy season.'[27]

The work the men had to undertake on the railway also became harder during the monsoon: 'The downpour soon turns the camp into one big quagmire,' wrote Otto Kreefft, 'latrines are overflowing, food supplies dwindle even further and the sick and death rates increase. Because of the incessant rains the embankments have subsided and the work is getting behind schedule.'[28]

'Another half a dozen of us were sent up just beyond Kanu to lay some lines. The "Speedo" was on at full pressure and this particular section lagged. We marched along the newly laid track past Kanu, a shambles of rotting tents and decaying bamboo huts which spewed out rotting and decaying bodies only distinguishable from corpses because they breathed and moaned for water.'[29]

50

is how many feet the level of the Khwae Noi can rise during the monsoon. The POWs at Brankassi had no knowledge of this and were taken completely by surprise when the monsoon hit. When they arrived at the camp **208** kilometres from Bam Pong in the dry season, they built a cookhouse out of bamboo close to the river so that the cooks had a ready supply of water. At that time of the year the Khwae Noi was at its lowest level, but when the monsoon began the river started to rise. In one night alone it rose **20** feet and the men had to move the cookhouse in the dark. This happened three times as the river rose to a height of around **50** feet.[30]

Another consequence of the monsoon was that the deluge was so heavy that as soon as the grave diggers dug a hole for burial it filled up with water. It was also difficult to burn the bodies with wet wood and no petrol was available as an accelerant.

During the monsoon the latrines at many of the camps overflowed. Kanchanaburi was one such place, as Arthur Godman recalled: 'When the rains came the latrines started to fill up with water and very soon the contents approached the top of the trench. The sewage was a seething mass of maggots which did not cause much concern during the dry weather because the level was a good five feet below the surface. But with the rains the maggots started to crawl over your feet as you squatted on the bamboo poles laid across the trench on which we had to squat.'[31]

The site of what used to be Kui Yae POW cemetery, then and now. By mid-October 1943, **62** of the **100** Australians who arrived in August were dead.

The Colonel of Tamarkan – Lieutenant Colonel (later Brigadier) Philip Toosey CBE, DSO, TD, JP, LLD – photographed in 1942. It was the men under his command who helped build the famous bridge over the Khwae Yai River at Kanchanaburi. (*Copyright: The Toosey Family Collection*)

The latrines at Takanun camp were originally dug on an isthmus which projected out into the Khwae Noi. Unfortunately, when the monsoon arrived, the water level rose so high in the river and the maggots which were living on top of the latrines were washed onto those prisoners sleeping nearby. Eventually, the entire isthmus was swept away.[32]

It was the latrines throughout the camps which left some of the most indelible impressions upon the POWs, such as those at Bam Pong, which Lieutenant Colonel Lionel Manning described as ghastly: 'insofar as it consisted of one enormous open trench filled to within eighteen inches of the top with excreta and which was crawling and seething with white maggots, which were the larvae of flies, and which crawled over one's boots.'[33]

At Songkurai during the height of the monsoon, one of the latrines which had filled up with rainwater, broke apart and a 'filthy stream oozed through the camp' and passed under the floors of the hospital huts and many of the sick bays collapsed.[34]

The torrential rains of the monsoons and the tough physical labour demanded of the POWs meant that their boots and uniforms quickly disintegrated, and few items of clothing were issued to the prisoners by the Japanese. At a camp of **2,200** men all that was received was **40** pairs of cheap rubber boots, **20** pairs of shorts and **10** shirts about every **2** months. Most of the prisoners were reduced to wearing just a short Japanese loincloth.[35]

The Australian official history lists what an average prisoner's possessions were during the early days of the monsoon/speedo period in addition to the loincloth. These usually consisted of an old hat, a water bottle, with or without cork, a mess tin and spoon, a leaky foul-smelling groundsheet, **2** sacks or perhaps a thin blanket, a pack to carry the equipment in, and possibly a share in a mosquito net. The lucky ones still had a pair of boots with leaking soles, but no socks.[36]

4

At the base camps near the terminus of the railway at both the Thailand and Burma ends, food was more plentiful than at the camps deep in the jungle. At the Thailand terminus, Non Pladuc, in addition to the standard ration, the prisoners were able to buy many extra items from the camp canteen. Such items were coffee, bananas, fried eggs, omelettes, fudge, roasted peanuts, jam tarts and meat pies. Strangely, the Japanese checked each order and only permitted the prisoners to purchase **4** items a day.

The Japanese Quartermaster, named Oda, demanded **3** per cent of the gross price of each item sold. This, he claimed, would be spent for the benefit of the prisoners. This continued for **8** months until it was suddenly stopped without explanation. No refund was given and no purchases were made with the money for the POWs. The average amount handed over each month was **300** dollars.[37]

So many of the former POW camps have been left untouched by the Thais. This is where the largely Dutch camp of Brankassi was situated.

30

is how many days punishments could last, Major W. E. Gill reported at Nong Pladuk camp. The usual punishment handed out by the Japanese was for the unfortunate prisoners to be forced to stand to attention outside the guard room, regardless of the weather, be it under the baking sun or the lashing rain of the monsoon, which could last for up to **30** days. The prisoners would be allowed to sit down for **10** minutes every hour. If a prisoner fell to the ground he was beaten back onto his feet. On one occasion, **37** officers were made to stand without relief all night for mistakenly dismissing a parade too early.[38]

There seemed to be no limits to the inventiveness of the Japanese and Koreans in devising novel punishments. Beyond the normal beatings, more serious offences could lead to a spell in a cramped solitary confinement cell (often known as the 'no good house'), or being forced to stand with a heavy stone held above the head. A more sadistic punishment was to tie a POW to a stake and place a tin filled with stones or water around the neck, pulling the head down. Attempts to raise the head resulted in the jagged top of the tin cutting into the chest.

7,006

was the weight in kilogrammes of carbolic soap sent by the Swiss Red Cross to POWs in **9** shipments of items between November 1943 and July 1945. Switzerland was the Protecting Power for the British, American and Australian prisoners. (A Protecting Power is a neutral country that can look after the affairs of each of two warring nations).

The Japanese did not recognise the protecting powers in areas under their control so delegates from the protecting powers were not allowed to visit POW camps. The representative of the Geneva-based International Committee of the Red Cross (ICRC) in Thailand, Mr Werner Salzmann, was permitted to travel freely around the country but not in his official capacity nor was he permitted to enter any area under Japanese military control.

On 1 May 1943, Salzman received a telegram from Geneva asking him to buy supplies for distribution to the prisoners working on the railway. After approaching the Thai government and being told he had to deal directly with the Japanese, he finally received permission to send items to the prison camps

The site of the former camp of Tarsao, or Tha Sao. Thia was a very large HQ camp situated by the road leading up alongside the railway towards Burma and close to the Khwae Noi.

in September 1943. To help him gauge how much he should purchase, Salzman asked the Japanese authorities how many prisoners they were holding, he was told that information was 'secret'. The wording of the agreement allowing 'money and comforts' to be sent to the prisoners was for just British PoWs but was meant to infer British Commonwealth soldiers as well. Among the items sent to the 'British' were:

10,761 kilogrammes of washing soap
31,000 toothbrushes
9,206,400 cigarettes
54,750 boxes of pipe tobacco
2,576 tins of Ovaltine, Bovril, and Marmite
7,416 tins of jam
7,720 kilogrammes of marmalade
8,064 tins of green peas and **9,840** kilogrammes of dried green peas
7,152 bottles of tomato sauce
5,206 tins of sardines and **26,500** tins of mackerel in oil
43,722 pounds of tea leaves
10,800 kilogrammes of roasted ground coffee

42,339 kilogrammes of sugar
28,008 1-pound tins of powdered milk and **2,736** tins of condensed milk
13,636 kilogrammes of peanuts
9,975 kilogrammes of ham
3,840 tins of biscuits
21,000 kilogrammes soya beans

Winston Churchill would, no doubt, have been pleased to learn that the prisoners were also sent **650,000** cigars. In total, the value of items sent was **2,668,556** baht.[39]

Few of the items sent by the Red Cross found their way to the POWs, the Japanese usually helping themselves before handing over what was left to the prisoners. Part of the problem being that **75** per cent of the goods were transported on normal troop trains going from Bangkok to Burma where they could easily be looted.

At Nong Pladuk it was noted that **248** of the **380** parcels from the American Red Cross were seized and shared by **75** to **100** Japanese guards, leaving just **82** parcels for the rest of the camp

A road was built roughly parallel with the railway to allow supplies to be transported up to the working areas. This was built by the PoWs. Malay Hamlet camp was situated on both sides of this road, which can be seen to the right of this photograph of the Malay Hamlet site. The road is now number 323.

population of **2,400**. This precise number was ascertained by the guards themselves who later handed over **248** tins of Cup Kafe which they said they disliked, the evidence from the parcels the prisoners did receive which included **1** such tin in each parcel. A total of **150** pairs of shorts were issued to the Japanese at Nong Pladuk and just **25** to the prisoners.[40]

In another instance in 1944, the Japanese commandant of Changaraya camp seized the supply of lint from an American Red Cross delivery from which he made, or had made for him, **3** pairs of pyjamas and a set of curtains for his hut.[41] Colonel Toosey at Nong Pladuc camp noted that in delivery parcels intended for individuals had to be shared among **10** men and in a later delivery each parcel had to be shared between **20** men. At Tarsao camp, though Red Cross supplies had been received, the Japanese did not hand the items out to the prisoners. It was noted that while the prisoners went barefoot, leather boots sat in the Japanese Quartermaster's store where they rotted in the hot and humid conditions or were eaten by rats. Much of that which did find its way to the POWs was sold to them by the Japanese.[42]

The extent to which goods had been withheld was demonstrated after Japan capitulated in September 1945, when large stocks of American items destined for the prisoners were released from Bangkok where they had been sitting for **15** months.[43]

During the monsoon, the supply road became impassable. This truck is stuck in the mud near the Three Pagodas Pass.

The Protecting Power for the Dutch POWs was Sweden. The Dutch prisoners received two shipments through the Swedish Red Cross, one in October 1944 and the other in May/June 1945. Included in these shipments were:

8,800 kilogrammes of brown sugar
1,042 kilogrammes of tea 'dust'
3,600 1-pound tins of powdered milk
400 tins of Ovaltine
3,600 kilogrammes of soya beans
800 pounds of margarine
600,000 cigarettes
8,600 boxes of pipe tobacco

18 cents was the cost per man per day of a new diet introduced for POWs at Tarsau on 22 November 1943. This was composed of soft rice porridge with sugar and tea with sugar for breakfast; sweet white sauce for elevenses; salted vegetable soup, again with a mug of sweet tea, for lunch and another serving of sweet white sauce in the afternoon around 15.00 hours. The evening

Inside one of the huts at Kanchanaburi in 1944 (*AWM P01502.006*)

meal was salted soup, rice pudding pap with sugar, and tea with sugar. A last mug of sweet tea was issued at 20.00 hours.

A 'special' diet was also introduced at this time for those undergoing surgery or whose dysentery or oedema were considered to be critical, which cost **30** cents per patient per day. This was a breakfast of porridge with sugar, a vegetable rissole and a boiled or poached egg, rice and a mug of tea. Lunch was vegetable soup with tripe or liver or fish and rice. This was followed by an undefined 'sweet' and tea. At 16.00 hours the patients received one-eighth of a tin of milk and a sweet biscuit. The evening meal was vegetable soup again with rice but also included meat 'with blood', and a fried egg. To finish, they had fruit, if available, and a mug of tea.[44]

1,000 was the price in Thai baht in 1945 for aspirin on the black market. The government price was just **50** baht. In 1943, the government price had also been **50** baht and **120** baht on the black market but such was the demand due to the influx of so many workers on the railway, and disruption to supply caused by the war, other medicines desperately needed in the hospitals of the POW camps along the railway saw similar rates of inflation. Ether, which cost **50** baht from the Thai Government in 1944,

A Japanese soldier stands on guard near the entrance to the POW camp at Thanbyuzayat, Burma, in late 1942 or 1943.

was sold on the black market for a staggering **1,300** baht and Sulphanilamide which was sold by the government for **90** baht could be obtained on the black market for **700** baht in 1943 but cost **12,000** baht in 1945.[45]

Inflation affected most items which the Thais sold to the prisoners, taking advantage of the desperation of the men and the unique bargaining position the Thais were in. At Tarsao camp, for example, eggs went from **7** cents each in 1942 to **25** cents each in 1945.[46]

8½

It was rare for the Japanese to issue any clothing or footwear to the POWs, and when they did provide IJA rubber slippers, the largest size was **8½**.

50

Corporal Yukichi Ishii was at Tampi camp when it was noticed that **50** tins of cooked beef and **10** tins of bacon were missing from the Japanese storeroom. A jute bag with an English name was found at the scene of the crime. The Japanese located the prisoner in question but saw that he was suffering from malaria and was clearly incapable of stealing anything. In the usual Japanese fashion, they began to 'extract' from him the name of the culprit. As things were about to get nasty, one of the POWs came forward and confessed to the crime. The prisoner was taken before the camp commander who merely told the **5** guards to deal with the man as they saw fit. After some discussion, the guards decided that the punishment would be that he should be hit on the backside **50** times. Taking it in turns, they hit him with their fists, administering the full **50** strikes.[47]

800

In November 1942 some **800** Koreans were employed on the railway as engineers and guards. They were recruited with the offer of **50** yen per month. They were taught the same doctrine as the Japanese soldiers – that discipline was maintained through corporal punishment and any error or sign of dissent was dealt with by being physically beaten and being seen by others to have received such punishment to act as a deterrent to others. They were instructed in this during their training, as one of the Korean guards (Army Civilian Employee Lee Han-ne) explained:

Australian POWs in Kanchanaburi, chopping and sawing wood in front of the cookhouse. (*AWM P01502.001*)

'The training included marching, rifle shooting and fighting with bayonets, and the most remarkable thing for us was that we were slapped on the cheek very often for even a minor error or misconduct. Sometimes everybody in the group was slapped for a mistake made by one person, or we had to stand in two lines facing each other and slap the comrade in front of us.'[48]

Such disciplinary methods applied at all levels. For instance, the Japanese commander of all POWs in Burma 'bashed' his second-in-command until he lost his footing and then kicked him down a set of stairs, causing a severe injury to the second-in-command's back. For injuring his back, the second-in-command was then sent in disgrace to a POW working camp where he stayed in hospital for **6** weeks under the care of a POW medical officer.[49]

1 So extreme was the degree of discipline that when standing to attention in front of a Japanese soldier should a prisoner's heels be **1** inch apart, he would be severely beaten.[50]

This form of discipline manifested itself sometimes, seemingly to Western eyes, illogically, as Gunner James Davie wrote: 'One of the Japanese in charge of the Korean guards was a Corporal whom we called "Tiger". We were forced by "Tiger" to carry sick prisoners out to work and he was always kicking and beating us. If we complained to him [about ill treatment we received from Korean guards], however, he promptly kicked them and beat them.'[51]

With, in many camps, just a handful of teenage guards controlling hundreds of prisoners, the guards felt they had to be firm with the POWs or they would lose control, which explains why they slapped the prisoners at the first sign of perceived dissension. Some of the Koreans, who were considered as an inferior race by the Japanese, took sadistic pleasure in exercising the authority they wielded over the prisoners.

One of the most notorious of these was Toyoyama Kisei. He famously carried a steel-shafted golf club which he used to beat prisoners with. There was no apparent rational to his attacks. On one afternoon he might hit **4** or **5** prisoners and then not strike anyone for a week.

A typical incident regarding Toyoyama was recorded at Ban Pong, when Major Roderick Anderson was staging through the camp with his party of **400** prisoners when Toyoyama demanded a roll call, or *tenko*. Anderson gave his count to Toyoyama. As this figure, though correct, did not correspond to Toyoyama's, he struck Anderson over the head with the golf club.[52]

One day in the late summer of 1943, Private D.S. Pickard of 2/30 Australian Infantry Battalion, saw two British POWs washing in the guards' area of the little creek which supplied Kami (Upper) Songkurai camp. This was upstream of the POW area and was divided from the POW area by a log. Toyoyama came along and saw the two prisoners. 'He became enraged,' recalled Pickard, 'stood them to attention, picked up a handful of mud and made them eat it. The mud was full of maggots and rotten rice due to all the camp food containers being washed in this area.'[53]

25

In the camps, even the lowest private considered himself the Emperor's representative and so it was mandatory for the prisoners, regardless of rank, to salute every Japanese soldier and even every Korean guard. In some camps it was also mandatory for the POWs to bow as well. Failure to follow these procedures would result in being slapped in the face or even beaten with a stick. In Kanchanaburi camp a Japanese sergeant passed by a group of **25** British and Commonwealth officers and was not seen by the group, so the usual salute was not given. On this excuse the entire group was made to stand at attention bareheaded in the sun before the Japanese guard house from 11.00 hours until 15.00 hours. Several fainted from sunstroke and were left there where they fell.

At Konyu camp an officer was struck in the face with a stick by the guard because he had failed to salute him. The officer in question had very poor eyesight – indeed his spectacles were knocked off and broken when he was hit – and, remarkably, the guard was made to pay for the repair of the glasses.

In another instance, an Australian officer was 'savagely' attacked by a Korean guard with heavy faggots of wood for failing to salute him even though, at the time, the guard was naked and covered in soap in a bathhouse.[54]

Though the camp commanders had absolute authority within the camp, they had none beyond it. This was how the IJA operated. An extreme example of this was given in a Foreign Office report: 'In the middle of 1944, a small party of POWs is sent upline. They passed the night at Tarsao and were called to the Japanese kitchen to get their meal there. A train with Japanese wounded from Burma arrived. Some of the wounded came to the kitchen to ask for some food. The Japanese NCO in charge chased them away to "go somewhere else to die" and cooly went on distributing food to the POWs.' The reasoning given for this is that the POWs were part of the NCO's unit, over which he had both authority and responsibility, whereas the soldiers were someone's responsibility.[55]

173,225 was the number of letters from friends and relatives sent to the prisoners in the camps in Thailand by a group of POWs in Changi Gaol, Singapore. The Japanese mail distribution system was so badly run, the prisoners stepped in to help. Calling itself the 'Bureau of Record and Enquiry', it sorted out **128** bags of mail containing **472,275** letters. These were repackaged into **52** bags for **22** different locations, of which **27** were destined for Thailand.[56]

Tamarkan camp in 1945.

23

was how many months some letters took from being posted in the UK to being received by the prisoners. In one recorded example **234** letters were sent by one POW's wife and children from 25 June 1942 to 10 August 1944. The first of these was received **20** months later in February 1944 and one sent in August 1943 was not received until August 1945.[57]

Periodically, the prisoners themselves were issued cards by the Japanese to allow them to write home. Except under special circumstances these had to be addressed to a relative with the same last name as the sender. The cards were pre-written, and all the prisoners were permitted to do was cross out the sentences which did not apply:

I am interned in Thailand
My health is excellent
I am ill in hospital
I am working for pay
I am not working
Please see that ....is taken care of

My love to you.
(Signature)

5

cents is how much a rat's tail was worth. At the most northerly of the Kinsaiyok camps the Japanese were very worried about the great hordes of rats which infested the camp getting at their foods, so they had a deep ditch dug around their store. They also offered the prisoners **5** cents for every rat's tail they brought to them. In their efforts to get to the food store the rats dropped into the ditch where they were chased and killed by the POWs. In the course of little more than **3** days, the Japanese were presented with around **2,500** rats' tails. Such was the success of this measure, the whole camp was turned out to kill rats and by the end of **6** weeks some **10,000** had been killed. There was a further benefit to this rat hunt in that typhus, of which there were periodic outbursts, is thought to have been transmitted through the bite of rats' fleas.

100

is how many flies prisoners were ordered by the Japanese to kill each day using improvised fly swats at Nam Chon Tai camp. The daily 'catch' was checked by the guards each evening and then destroyed.[58] Flies were a major problem at all the camps and at some of them measures were put in place to combat this menace. At Tamarkan, Colonel Toosey arranged for the camp carpenters to make baited fly-traps, and he organised mass 'fly hunts' giving a prize each day for the largest number of flies caught which were taken to him personally each evening in a tin. He also noted that 'there even became a black market in dead flies.'

60

Near Wampo Central, a camp for sick POWs living in poor conditions cared for by just a few orderlies, were some **60** fit young officers, whom Ian Denys Peek, a member of the Singapore Volunteers, complained, stayed out of sight in their own hut, sitting 'around on their bums all day, playing bridge and reading and complaining about not being able to get decent pipe tobacco.'[59]

Such complaints were not uncommon. At the large Tarsao camp, for instance, officers were separated from the other ranks in their own compound where they had their own messes and enjoyed dinners, went bathing in the river and even had their own latrines. Lieutenant John Durnford also mocked the appearance of his fellow officers' faces, which he said bore an unhealthy pallor because they never saw the sun, 'sheltered behind enclosures with palm-thatched walls at their entrances. Within these, officers took the evening air rather as they might on the veranda of a permanent station mess.'[60]

Of course, there were very many cases where officers worked inside or outside the camps and numerous examples of heroic officers being brutally treated for defending their men.

100

An all-officer work party was formed at Chungkai to work in a vegetable garden outside the camp, the best produce of which was to go, predictably, to the Japanese. The officers protested, stating that though they could volunteer, they should not be forced to work, and asked that the work be regarded as 'voluntary' The Japanese agreed to this face-saving compromise and **100** 'volunteers' were ordered to begin work under their own leaders.

As well as the main camps, there were a number of temporary sub-camps where conditions were often even worse than the main camps from where the prisoners had been moved. Such camps did not have the administrative or medical support of the main camps. One such was a temporary working camp adjacent to Hintok camp. At this place, out of **500** British soldiers, **155** died in just **6** weeks.[61]

25th of December 1943, Christmas Day was celebrated throughout the camps with the Japanese permitting the troops a day off from any work. Typical of the celebrations were those at Tarsau, where the prisoners had been preparing for the big day for weeks beforehand. The cooks had been hoarding food to provide a special meal for lunch and a bamboo stage had been built upon which was delivered a performance of *Cinderella* – though the legs of the 'ladies were marred by septic scars and tropical ulcers'. The hospital was 'thronged' with visitors taking little gifts and improvised Christmas cards. There was, of course, a service led by the padre, and in the evening, there was a lottery and, of course, a visit from Father Christmas.

Concerts and theatrical events were commonplace in many of the camps before and, more frequently, after the speedo period.

In an early concert at Hlepauk in Burma, a Dutchman, who was a professional magician, put on a show. A few of the natives from the nearby *rŏmusha* camp attended the concert but when the magician performed a trick in which a handkerchief seemingly danced in the air, the terrified *rŏmusha* ran back to their camp.

The Japanese at Wampo also put on their own show for the sake of the prisoners, watched by John Godber: 'They sang a lot of very tuneless songs with great gusto, several of them gave little acts of their own such as dancing & general buffoonery. They also sang "Auld Lang Syne" for which they have their own words and "She'll be coming round the mountain when she comes" – a Jap version of the English words.'[62]

4 was the width in metres of ditches which the POWs had to dig around each camp in October 1944. The ditches were also **3** or **4** metres deep. As the war turned against the Japanese, relations between the Japanese and their captives became increasingly tense. Fearing an uprising by the Allied prisoners, in January 1945, the officers were segregated from their men and placed in a camp at Kanchanaburi.

The camps, which had been comparatively open up to this date, were surrounded with barbed wire and bamboo fences. Sentry posts were built and placed so as to cover the entire boundary of the camp. Orders were issued that any POW seen near the ditch would be shot on sight. At many camps a bank was also built outside the ditch which was patrolled by Japanese sentries. Harsh rules were imposed at this time. It was forbidden to smoke outside and was only permitted inside the accommodation huts providing the prisoners had both feet on the ground. Except at certain limited times, reading books or lying down was forbidden.

All contact with the locals ceased and any attempt to do so was met with severe punishment. Lieutenant R. G. Martin in the Officers' Camp at Kanchanaburi was accused of looking through the perimeter fence and was made to stand to attention outside the Japanese guardhouse for **4** days.

Chapter 4

Disease and Death

45 is the total number of diagnosed illnesses suffered by the POWs during their time in captivity. The most common diseases were malaria, dysentery, beriberi, pellagra, ulcers and oedema, but the list also included hernias, fractures, appendicitis and 'mental derangement'.[1] Fractures, sprains and soft-tissue injuries were common everywhere, related both to the railway work (e.g. blast injuries, falls from bridges etc), and to beatings and punishments by the Japanese and Korean guards.[2]

Sergeant Seiichi Okada, often called 'Doctor Death' by the prisoners, set standards for the men with dysentery. If they had '**10**' motions a day, they were fit for duties in the camp. At **20** motions, they 'perhaps' could do some light work, but he accepted that at **30** motions or more a day they were genuinely unfit for work of any description. According to another report, Okada had a 'hatred' of sick people and would often beat patients with his fists as they laid helplessly on their beds (TNA WO 311/547). He was later sentenced to **10** years imprisonment (*AWM P00634.005*)

12 was the number of bandages issued each month by the Japanese for the **500** prisoners at Hlepauk, 18 Kilo camp, where all the medical staff except **1** and **2** orderlies were made to work on the railway. The POWs were unable to take much in the way of medical stores with them when they were transported to Thailand and Burma and were reliant upon the Japanese to supply them with the necessary items. In addition to these few bandages, the Japanese issued some gauze, **1** kilogramme of magnesium sulphate and **100** aspirin tablets. Occasionally the medical staff would also be given a Japanese-produced ointment and a real 'luxury' in the form of tincture of iodine, which is an antiseptic. This was all that was provided for men suffering from all manner of tropical diseases.

Necessity, however, is the mother of invention, and the prisoners, who came from all walks of life with a wide range of skills, manufactured a huge range of items, mostly from the most abundant material available – bamboo – to help the medical teams, as this list of articles shows, the POWs providing or gathering the materials themselves: 'Artificial limbs, bedpans, charcoal pattern sterilizers of tin and mud, bowls, buckets, trays, brooms, pneumonia jackets, oil lamps, urine bottles, ladles, mugs, pillows and mattresses (rice sacks and straw), funnels, irrigating pans, fly-proof latrine lids, fly traps, leg rests, instrument boxes (bamboo), vegetable scrapers, clogs, stretchers, special beds, surgical and orthopaedic apparatus, pullies, even bamboo scalpels for crude dressing work and bamboo needles. Artificial eyes were carved from Mahjong pieces.'[3]

As part of the rehabilitation scheme for those men who had lost limbs a self-supporting arts and crafts 'industry' was set up manufacturing many of these items in some of the larger camps. The amputees also made clothes and repaired shoes.

23 is the percentage of deaths of POWs in camps in Thailand due to malaria in October 1943, the greatest single cause of death. Almost every prisoner caught at least one variant of malaria during their time on the railway. The medical records of one man, Private S. Dawson, indicate that he contracted malaria **30** times. Though mosquito nets and blankets were issued in some camps, they quickly disappeared, as one prisoner, Sergeant L. L. Baynes complained: 'There was unfortunately a lot of thieving from comrades going on in Chunkai camp ...Blankets, most valuable of all the captive's possessions, were stolen and sold to the Thais. With no protection from the malaria-carrying mosquito many must have died solely because of these camp thieves. Even the medical hut was broken into and our scanty supply of medicines robbed for private gain. Some became so wealthy that they were able to bribe those in charge to let them stay in camp as sick men, while the really sick were forced out to work.'[4] As many as **800–900** cases of malaria per month were being seen by the medical team at Chungkai.

In Burma in that same month, October 1943, it was dysentery which was the biggest killer, amounting to **38.3** per cent. This disease was due, of course, to the insanitary conditions in which the POWs lived – and, of course, the inadequate diet: 'In a wasting disease such as this,' wrote Lieutenant Colonel Huston, 'with food of limited caloric value, it was essential to use all means to make patients eat every grain of rice procurable for them otherwise they consumed their body proteins which on the diet could not be replaced.'[5] This was echoed by Lieutenant Colonel Coates: 'The route home is inscribed in the bottom of every man's dixie. Every time it is filled with rice, eat it. If you vomit it up again, eat some more; even if it comes up again some good will remain. If you get a bad egg, eat it no matter how bad it may appear. An egg is only bad when the stomach will not hold it.'[6]

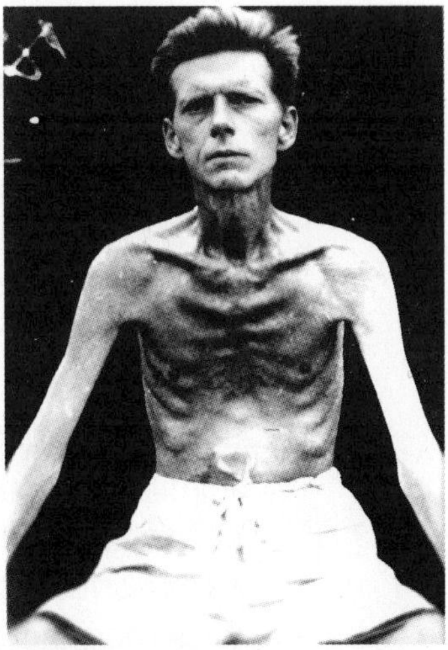

Sergeant M.A. Priest, Straits Settlements Volunteer Force, showing the effects of dysentery, (*AWM P01433.022*)

Dysentery was one of the illnesses which in some camps were considered debilitating to the extent that sufferers were not forced to go out to work on the railway. The more men who were unavailable for work put more pressure on those who had no choice but to work. It was essential, therefore, for the medical officers to weed out any malingerers and make sure only those who were genuinely ill remained in camp. In Konyu camp, Dr Stanley Pavilliard did this by insisting that those reporting with dysentery should bring a sample of their stools for examination carried on, for example, a leaf. It was not long before the doctor became suspicious – the stools were beginning to look familiar. He discovered that there was indeed 'a brisk trade' in genuine dysentery stools! For a little money or some cigarettes, dysentery sufferers were selling their stools. To tackle this problem, Pavilliard demanded the claimants produced their stools in his presence. Consequently, of **300** men lining up, **90** entered the enclosure to produce stools, and only **17** turned out to be genuine dysentery patients. [7]

Mentioned often in the memoirs of prisoners, is a bizarre procedure widely adopted by the Japanese in response to an outbreak of dysentery, that of 'glass rodding' or 'bum-sticking'. Geoffrey Gill explains: 'This was a form of screening for the disease involving lining up large groups of POWs, who would then have to bend down whilst the Japanese inserted glass rods into their rectums, and took the rods away "for examination". The practice had no scientific validity then or now, and it was doubtful whether anything was actually done with these specimens.'[8]

The pointless nature of these exercises was confirmed by Private Harry Howarth: 'We were called out on parade for a medical inspection. We were even more astonished when we discovered the type of medical inspection. Eyebrows were raised when the Jap "medical orderly" who probably swept the floor in a Tokyo abattoir, produced a glass rod about 12 inches long from a cardboard box and with a flourish began to jab it in the direction of the man at the head of the column. As it dawned on this individual that he was about to be deflowered with a blunt instrument, he attempted to sneak away, but too late, he was seized, told to bend over, and the bloody great glass rod was inserted into his lower rectum. As the Japanese used the glass rods, there was no attempt at tabulation of any kind and all the glass rods were thrown together in the same box. It was obviously just a propaganda exercise so that they could say they had tested POWs for dysentery infection.'[9]

The fourth largest cause of death was beriberi which, as mentioned earlier, is due to a lack of vitamin B1. The effects of the disease were described by Dr Pavillard: 'We began to feel that our feet did not belong to us, that we were walking on cottonwool; at the same time the soles of the feet burned as if they were on fire. As the disease progressed, first the legs would start to swell, and then the swelling would travel upwards until in some cases the testicles looked like footballs. Sometimes the disease attacked the nervous system, and we lost muscular control of our feet.'[10] Eventually, death would occur from heart failure. In 'F' Force, **413** died of beriberi, of which **279** were British, and **134** were Australians. The peak of beriberi deaths in 'F' Force was November 1943 when there were **111** deaths.

Yet in death, men gave hope to the living after Brigadier Varley announced in November 1942 that the personal effects of the dead would be sold and the proceeds paid into a Red Cross fund to buy food for the sick. These included such items as watches and fountain pens. Only wallets and photographs were to be retained to be sent to next of kin when the force eventually returned home.

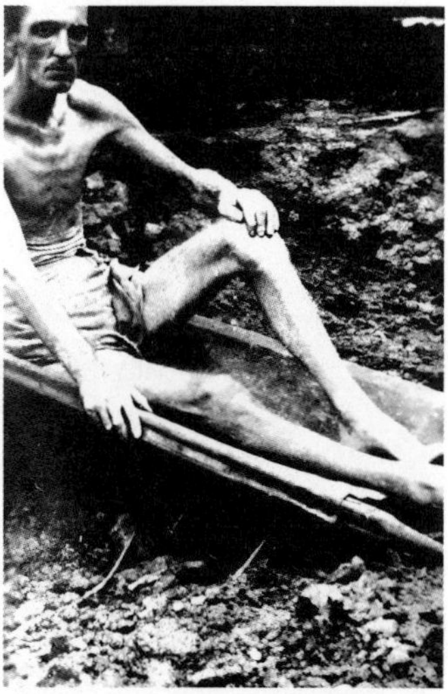

Gunner J. P. Bradley showing the effects of malaria and beriberi. He had suffered 6 bouts of malaria in 6 weeks, three of which were without quinine. During this period, he was only able to complete one day's work and was kicked by a Japanese soldier who broke his ribs. (*AWM P01433.024*)

Recording the cause of death proved challenging for the Allied doctors. There were a number of reasons for this. The first one was that patients often suffered from more than one disease any one of which could, in itself, prove fatal. The true cause was malnutrition, but the Japanese did not permit that to be recorded. The second problem was the lack of paper and pens to record the diseases the patients had. What case records the medics had, were often written in pencil on scraps of paper which, in time, became faded and illegible. Eventually, where possible, individual medical

Three 'fit' workers at Shimo Songkurai No 1 Camp, standing outside the camp hospital. Identified, left to right, believed to be: NX4417 Bruce Pearce, NX47506 Oscar Jackson, and NX47513 Reuben Niles Pearce, all of the 2/30th Battalion. The prisoner at right is unable to fasten his shorts because his stomach is swollen with beriberi. (*AWM P02569.192*)

cards were made out of tobacco and cigarette packets and given to the men to keep as their personal medical record.

5

The deadliest disease encountered in the regions through which the railway was built was cholera. On 15 May 1943, **5** cases of cholera were diagnosed among a party of Australians which had moved from Konkoita camp to Lower Nikhe camp. At almost the same time, cholera had been identified at other camps. This marked the start of a devastating and deadly epidemic which swept through the camps. The disease took a grip on its victims with shocking rapidity. So frequent was the vomiting and the defecation within just a few hours the individuals became so dehydrated they died – usually within **24** hours of the first signs of the illness. Many are the accounts of a man becoming ill one day and being dead the next, some not even making it through the night.

This was directly attributable to the criminal negligence of the Japanese, complained Major Cyril Wild. 'For at Konkuita [*sic*], the last staging camp but two, every one of the thirteen marching parties was forced to camp for one or more days within a few yards of huts filled with hundreds of cholera-stricken coolies and on ground covered with infected faeces, where the air was black with flies. British officers asked for the loan of spades to remove this filth but the Japanese replied contemptuously, "use your hands".'[11]

The cause of cholera in the region is found in the huge rise and fall of the River Khwae. During the dry season the water level drops to such an extent that a mass of decaying vegetation, dead animals, and waste from villages upstream, is deposited on the exposed riverbanks. This rots in the hot sun and becomes a breeding ground for all manner of bacteria, including cholera. When the monsoon rains swell the river, these deadly bacteria are swept into the water.

Consequently, as soon as the medical personnel in a camp were alerted to a breakout of the disease a number of preventative measures were put in place. These were that only boiled water should be used for drinking and brushing teeth and that all eating and cooking utensils should be dipped in boiling water before use. Bathing in the river was prohibited and any food touched by flies or ants had to be thrown away – a measure which must have caused anguish among the hungry prisoners and was impossible to enforce. The men were also warned not to lick paper when they rolled up their cigarettes.

Ian Denys Peek was stationed at the POW camp most severely affected by the 1943 cholera outbreak, Tonchan South. He described the awful nature of the disease: 'The symptoms are frequently violent, fluid of greyish-white colour being ejected forcefully in vomiting and diarrhoea as if the kidneys are trying to rid the body of invasive poisons. The result is rapid dehydration with accompanying muscular cramps of such intensity that the muscle fibres can tear apart as the body writhes and twists in wrenching spasms.'[12]

At most of the camps, a separate, quarantined area was quickly established at a distance from the main camp to hold the cholera victims, referred to in many camps as 'Cholera Gulch'. One such named area was at Hintok Valley camp, which was a 'dismal flooded area' a short distance away from the main camp. Jeffery English saw the cholera tents which were 'frightful beyond description'. 'The blotched, stinking emaciated victims lay packed like sardines twenty or thirty to a tent, occasionally groaning or twitching into activity and crying feebly for orderlies with bedpans, but most of them lying quite still.'[13]

Captain Harry Silman, a Medical Officer with the 9th Northumberland Fusiliers, recorded a similar scene at Changaraya: 'I have been over to the cholera centre. It looks like a scene from a film, completely unreal. There is a long, dark, attap hut, with over a hundred thin skeleton-like beings, writhing on the long platform, vomiting and passing motions where they lie. Groans and cries are the only noises to break the silence ...About nine corpses lay outside covered with blankets and groundsheets, and a little distance away, the smoke of the pyre where the corpses are burning could be seen.'[14]

70

was the percentage death rate of cholera victims at Songkurai camp between 21 May and 26 June 1943. During this period there were **315** admissions with cholera to the camp hospital, with **219** deaths, representing that shocking mortality rate of **70** per cent.[15]

At Tamarkan camp the outbreak of cholera saw an immediate response from the Japanese, as noted by Sergeant Fred Seiker: 'Overnight the huts were filled with the dead and the dying. The Japs were terrified of this disease and hastily retreated to a safe distance up the road after barricading the entrance to the camp with X-shaped barricades and rolls of razor wire.'

Such was the fear the Japanese had of the disease, when cholera struck Takanun camp in the middle of May 1943, the first step the Japanese took was to erect a bamboo fence between their area of the camp and that of the prisoners. Anyone entering the Japanese area had to wipe their feet on a disinfectant-soaked sack which was held in a box at the gate. They then had to wash their hands in an adjacent bowl of disinfectant.

The bodies of those who had died had to be burned, with up to **10** being cremated at a time. Private Fred Whalley wrote of the funeral pyres towards the end of the cholera outbreak at Konyu II

Despite the frequency of deaths, as much dignity as was possible was shown to each prisoner who died. The body was sewn into a grey Army blanket and carried to the cemetery on a rice sack suspended between bamboo poles. A bugle played The Last Post and Reveille. During the cholera outbreak, however, the bodies were burned on mass funeral pyres. (*AWM P00406.031*)

Camp: 'These fires flared at every camp where cholera struck. They lighted the way out to work in the dark before dawn, they guided the men back through the dark wetness of the jungle long after dusk. And always, lying around them in stick-like bundles were the bodies that awaited cremation – bodies at which the returning men peered closely as they came in, to see if any of their mates lay among them.'[16]

Private E. S. Benford was in one of the parties responsible for cremating the cholera victims: 'It was the most horrible, nauseating task I had encountered. We had no masks and we knew that we must not on any account put our hands to our faces. I stood rooted to the spot, trying hard not to breathe, for the stench was sickening. The ghastly stench from hundreds of dead bodies, black wasted bodies, with their skeleton-like limbs spread grotesquely at every angle ...Each body was lying in a pool of grey liquid vomit and excreta. Flies swarmed over the bodies in their millions and set up a continuous humming. I vomited over the first one that we tried to lift.'[17] Eventually, the Japanese, who objected to the smell of the burning bodies, ordered the dead to be buried, and, in many instances, they were placed in mass graves.

It is said that at 85 Kilo Camp, when cholera broke out, **15** suspected cases of the disease along with **5** who had plague were isolated in **2** huts on a hill about **1** mile from the camp hospital. No one was allowed to go near them and no medicines, no water or food was given. It is understood all died either of illness or starvation. Later the Japanese burned the cholera hut down.[18]

Official figures of confirmed cases of cholera released by the Japanese, including native workers, were given as follows, though these statistics are considerably less than the true numbers as the Japanese failed to maintain accurate records. This was particularly the case with the Asiatic workers, large numbers of whom died unrecorded and unrecognised in the jungle. Though cholera was quite quickly eradicated in the POW camps due to the preventative measures taken, the disease was still present in the coolie population.

	1st Period	*Nov – Dec 1942*
2nd Period	Feb – March 1943	**48**
3rd Period	April – May 1943	**586**
4th Period	3 June – 30 June 1943	**2,046**
Total		**2,680**[19]

In Burma malaria took the highest toll. It was responsible for the death of **50** per cent of the patients. Tropical ulcers took the next **10** per cent, **20** per cent for beriberi and skin diseases. Still malaria took the highest toll of these diseases for Japanese Army and PoW personnel alike.

During the time that 9th Railway Regiment was in charge of construction in Thailand, a period of about **1** year the deaths were:

	Total	*Deaths*	*Percentage*
Labourers	Approx 45,000	**12,000**	**26**
PoWs	Approx 35,000	**6,000**	**17**
Japanese Army	Approx 2,600	**100**	**4**
Burmese Labourers	Approx 5,000	**3,500**	**7**

The reason why the figures are given as approximate is because the records of the two railway companies were destroyed at the end of the war.

1,000 is how many died at the large Chungkai camp since its opening in November 1942, this sad statistic being recorded on 31 March 1943. That month alone saw **255** deaths from all causes. The numbers had been slowly rising in the preceding months. In August it was **157** who had died, and in September it was **221**.

1,200 Songkurai was probably the worst camp of all. By May 1943, of the original **1,600** prisoners placed there, **1,200** had died and a further **200** were in hospital and unlikely to recover.[20]

The following numbers give an indication of the proportion of prisoners able to work compared with the total camp populations in July and August 1943:[21]

Camp	*Date*	*Camp Population*	*Sick*	*Number sent to work*
Shimo Songkurai	19 July	**1,850**	**1,350**	**345**
Takanun	mid-July	**564**	**404**	**160**
Songkurai	28 July	**1,300**	**1,050**	**280**
Kami Songkurai	16 August	**1,670**	**1,075**	**450**

Cholera Hill at Shimo Songkurai No 1 Camp. To the right of the hospital tents is a makeshift operating table where amputations, treatment for tropical ulcers and autopsies were done. (*AWM P02569.189*)

At the last camp on the above list, Kami Songkurai, during the period 3 August to 31 October, **1,965** Australians and **1,460** British were admitted to hospital, and **1,236** and **896** respectively discharged; deaths numbered **130** Australians and **195** British.

1,250 was the number of men who would be accommodated at a new hospital camp at Tanbaya in Burma. In July 1943, a project for the establishment of a hospital which could take the more seriously sick from the 'F' Force camps was put forward by the Japanese. The hospital was to accommodate **1,250** patients who were to be drawn from **2** categories. These were (a) men who would not recover from their present illness within two months, and (b) old men with a permanent disability or unsuited for heavy work on the railway.

The allotment of patients to camps was:

Nieke, **250**
Shimo-Songkurai, **500**
Songkurai, **350**
Kami-Songkurai, **50**
Changaraya, **100**

An advance party, consisting of an administrative team plus **8** medical officers and **36** other ranks of the medical staff assembled from the various camps, set off for Tanbaya on 30 July. After being forced to march part of the way as the railway was not in operation as a bridge had collapsed, the party reached Tanbaya on 3 August, **2** men having died on the journey.

Patients began arriving **5** days later in batches of between **30** and **120**. Of these. about **240** were suffering from tropical ulcers of varying degrees of severity, with or without complications. A special section of the hospital was allotted to these patients consisting of **2** wards capable of holding **180** and **160** patients. The treatment for tropical ulcers was often amputation and around **40** amputations took place at Tanbaya. Only **4** amputees survived.

One of the problems the camp staff had at Tanbaya was that of preventing patients from defecating and urinating just 'wherever and whenever they felt inclined,' complained Captain George W.

Gwynne, 'patients were often too lazy to call for a bedpan or at any rate to call early enough and would defecate through the slats of the bay. Others – sometimes light duty personnel would again through laziness defecate in the passage way or through the slats without any thought of their health or that of anyone else ...This filthy and dangerous practice was so bad at first that picquets with bamboo canes were mounted on latrines and in wards during the hours of darkness in an endeavour to compel troops to use the latrines and not the adjacent surroundings.'[22]

As the patients were only at Tanbaya because they were very ill, the death rate was high. The total number of deaths, including dead on arrival, up to 24 November was **665**, representing about **45** per cent of the British and **21** per cent of the Australian population of the camp.

Due to the large numbers of sick in each of the work camps, the Japanese decided to form base hospital camps to where those who were not likely to be in a fit state to work in the near future were sent. As those who did not work were not entitled, in Japanese eyes, to receive food or pay, each camp paid what it could to the hospital which received its men according to the number of sick the camp had sent.

10,000 is how many prisoner patients had been received at Chungkai towards the end of October 1943 in little over a year after it had been converted into a base hospital, and on the last day of that month the **1,000**th death had occurred at the camp.

19,975 is the total of how many patients were eventually treated at Chungkai Base Hospital, with around **2,000** men being treated in the hospital at any one time. Of this number of patients, **1,440** died, which was a mortality rate of **7.21** per cent.

Another of the base hospitals was Tarsau, which opened in November 1942 and closed in April 1944. It consisted of **24** 'rough tumbling bamboo and attap structures' reported Colonel Dunlop, 'with the usual rough continuous platforms of bamboo, one on either side of the building. The patients usually with their feet directed to the central pathway so that with the overcrowding, access to the sick patients was most difficult.' The peak mortality rate at Tarsau occurred in October 1943 when **83** died. During its time as a hospital it admitted **15,029** patients of whom **806** men died. It was noted that with no medicines available, many men would gradually sink into a 'final deficiency' state from which they would never recover. Such a state could last weeks before the patient finally died.

7

Despite the horrendous conditions at Tarsau, with death and disease all around the lack of decent food or medicines, there were, according to a report of 30 November 1943 only **7** cases of mental illness out of **2,407** patients.[23] Indeed, recorded cases of mental illness were rare. It is believed this was due, at least in part, to the 'stigmatisation and cultural unacceptability' of acknowledging such problems – and the effect this would have on morale. It seems those cases presenting with obvious psychiatric illnesses were quietly segregated.[24]

30

is how many died per day between October 1942 and March 1943 at a *rǒmusha* base hospital camp that was established at Dai Ni around **1** mile from Kanchanaburi. It consisted of **12** attap huts, each of which was around **200** feet long by **30** feet wide and held between **100** and **200** patients. These patients were **50** per cent Indian, **25** per cent Chinese and **20** per cent Malays or Thais. The balance was made up of British. Among the illness from which deaths occurred was typhoid. The bodies were buried in front of the hospital.

There was another *rǒmusha* hospital near Kanchanaburi at Dai Ichi. This was a larger hospital with some **2,000** patients held there at any one time. These hospitals were commanded by a Japanese medical officer but actually run by Allied doctors, though with the usual absence of medicines or medical equipment. [25]

40

was the number of men who survived from the **110** major amputations of legs carried out by Lieutenant Colonel Albert Coates at 55 Kilo Camp. One prisoner, Alf Mitchell, described the procedure: 'At the end of the hut you could see the Colonel operating. With the help of the Dutchman van Boxtel they had made a drug and they used it to stick in the back of your spine.

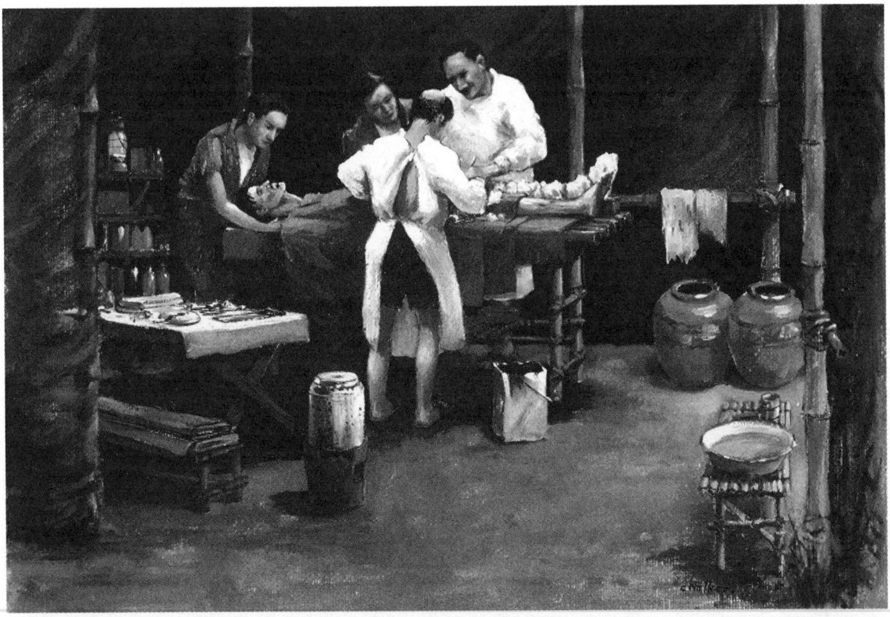

Colonel Edward 'Weary' Dunlop and Captain Jacob Markowitz working on a thigh operation at Chungkai.

The orderlies held your head and bent your back right over and stuck it in, which would paralyse you from the chest down. You could go there and watch ...Colonel would cut right around the flesh and he'd grip the arteries and that to stop the blood from flying out ...he was taking six legs a day off there.'[26]

Amputations were usually necessary due to the spread of tropical ulcers, which often began as mere scratches or small cuts to the legs or feet, though they could and did occur in almost any area of the body. After a few months most of the boots of the prisoners had worn out and they were forced to walk and work barefoot, and damage to feet and the lower parts of the legs was almost inevitable.

With no proper dressings, the men suffering cuts and abrasions on their way to and during work tried to cover the injuries with scraps of rags or even leaves in the hope of preventing the start of an ulcer. On return to camp in the evening the number needing attention was often so great that sick parades lasted till late at night.

The majority of ulcers spread with alarming speed, and a small, infected abrasion became within **48** hours a sloughing

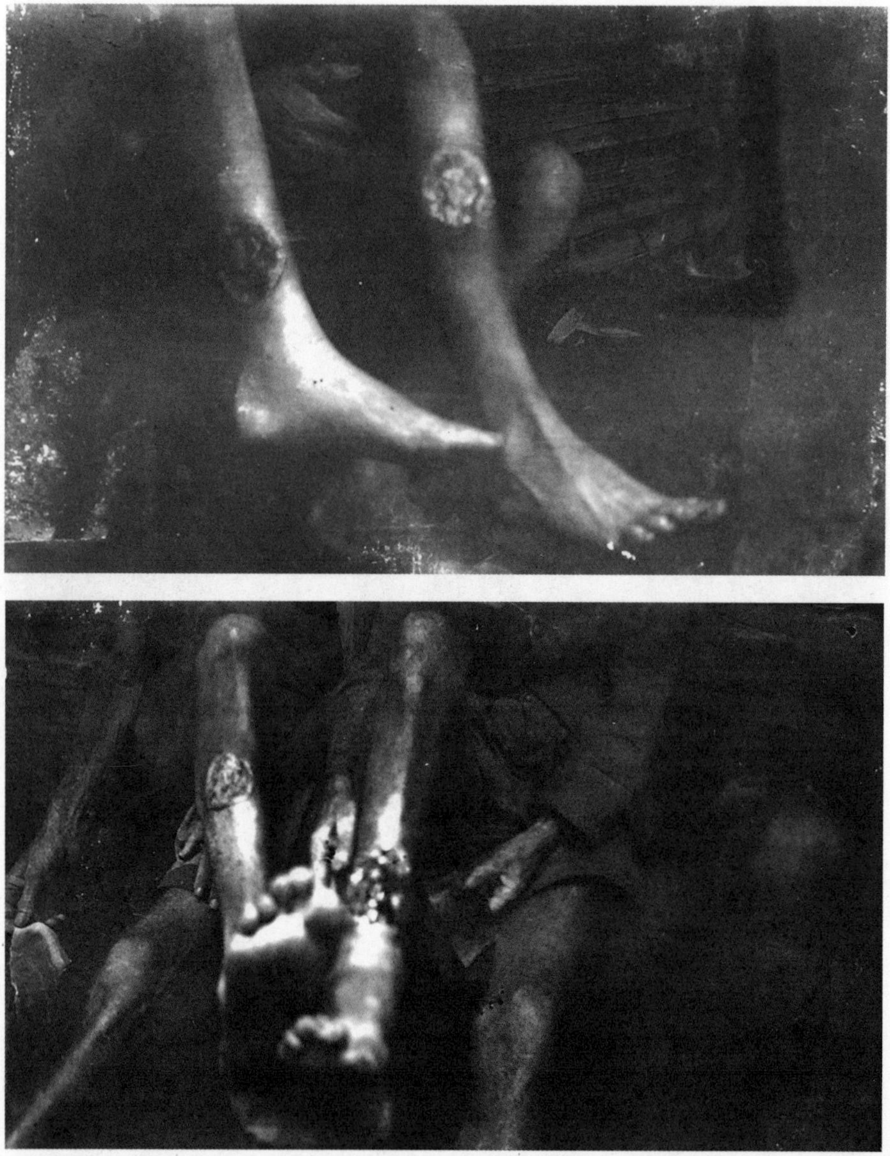

Tropical ulcers forming on the lower legs of two unidentified members of 'F' Force. (*AWM P02569.190*)

ulcer, eating away huge areas of skin, flesh, muscle and, in some cases bone. So common did ulcers become that at the hospital in Tha Makhan camp more than **500** cases were seen.

The routine treatment was frequent cleansing of the ulcers with hot water or saline. One of the treatments available at some of the camps was for the patients to wade into the river up to their waists. There they would stand while fish ate away the pus and the rotting flesh.[27] During the dry season, the water level in the river fell so low that men could sit on the pebbles on the bottom with their heads above the water.

If such treatments were not possible the affected matter would be scraped from the limb with a spoon, a terrifyingly painful procedure. Dick Ridgwell assisted the medical orderlies with this treatment at Tarsao hospital camp, 'and helped hold down those men while orderlies scraped away the maggoty pus from POWs' limbs using a silver spoon. This procedure was described by one of the prisoners: 'The orderly would dig his spoon firmly into the stinking pus until he had reached firm flesh and, having reached it, draw the spoon carefully down one side of the gaping wound and up the other. Swab it out: scoop out the few remaining mortified patches.'[28]

The pain was terrible for these patients. Following this appalling procedure doctors would take the torn blankets which had been sterilised in boiling water in nearby **44**-gallon drums placed over fires. These would be placed over the cleaned wound. This was the only procedure available for ulcer patients. There was nothing else.'[29]

Major Peter Campbell at Khonkan 55 Kilo camp, watched some of these procedures where four men would have to hold the patient down, the screams of the poor patients being 'nothing less than hair-raising'.[30]

Other than that concocted by van Boxtel, there was often little or no anaesthetics provided by the Japanese to help with pain relief during these operations but alcohol for surgical use was made by distillation of Burmese 'brandy', purchased through the camp commander and interpreter.

Despite the high mortality rate, patients willing submitted to the dreadful amputation process, as Captain Harry Silman experienced in September 1943: 'I saw my former batman, Windmill RE, today. He is in the ulcer ward, and looks a wreck of his former self. He pleaded with me with tears in his eyes for his leg to be taken off, but he is such a bad operative risk, I understand it will not be done. He says the pain is terrific, twenty-four hours a day, and at night he is afraid of losing his reason. What a terrible thing a tropical ulcer is.'[31]

Often, though, none of these procedures could halt the spread of the ulcers and at Tanbaya hospital camp **92** patients died of ulcers alone, and **105** of ulcers complicated by other diseases.

It was often the smell of the tropical ulcers which the prisoners remarked on. Typical of this are the words of Captain Ernest Gordon of the Argyll and Sutherland Highlanders when he described conditions at Chungkai hospital camp: 'The smell of tropical ulcers eating into flesh and bone; the smell as latrines overflowed; the smell of dirty men, untended men, sick men, of humanity rotting, humanity gone sour. Worst of all was the sweet, evil smell of bedbugs by the millions crawling over us to steal the little flesh that still clung to our bones.'

75 per cent of patients had scabies at Tarsau hospital camp. Though not fatal, this illness affected the prisoners throughout the camps and was caused by the vermin (called the 'minor horrors of war') that could never be effectively eliminated in their entirety with so many men squashed together in the huts and where the opportunity to wash was limited .[32]

365

was the number of medical personnel which were formed into 'K' and 'L' Forces that left Changi in June and August 1943 for Thailand to provide medical services for the workers including the *rŏmusha,* who were dying with no medical care in very large numbers. The medical teams were sent to Kanchanaburi, Wan Yai, Kinsaiyok, Konkoita and Neike.

One of those medical team members wrote of the conditions he witnessed in a transit camp: 'It was teeming with dying natives, all in the throes of dysentery and cholera. Coloured and white slept together in the same huts. Clad in rags or even naked, we huddled together during the cold wet nights. Natives and POWs were unable to control themselves, with vomit and excreta everywhere. Each day a number of POWs who could still walk were detailed to carry out those men and natives who had died during the night. The smell of death was everywhere, an almost sweet, sickly smell that defied description.' The medical teams reported on the intentional murders carried out by the Japanese on the *rŏmusha.*

The memorial plaque to 'Weary' Dunlop and the heroic work of the Allied medical officers.

500 is how many 'coolies' were buried at Neike by the medical teams in one mass grave. Unlike in the POW camps there was no hierarchy of command and therefore no disciple and no order or organisation. This was reflected in a report from the Labour Superintendent of Burmese Coolies on conditions he had seen at the camps between Thanbyuzayat and Kun Knit Kway: 'The coolies had many grievances and all beseeched me to help them to return to their homes. The working day lasted from 6 a.m. to 6 p.m. with one hour break for food. The sick were forced to work. They were often slapped and beaten. All the Japanese coolie overseers used to carry sticks for the purpose. Many labourers suffered with Cholera, Dysentery, Smallpox, Tropical Ulcers and Malaria. There were no doctors, no medical orderlies, no hospitals. The only medicine available was quinine. It was used as an ointment for ulcers and as sedative for dysentery and cholera. Food bad and insufficient. Inferior quality rice, some pumpkin and rotten, dried fish given once or twice a day.

'The bamboo huts were crowded, full of flies and vermin, leaking during rains. For trivial reasons the coolies were severely punished. They were tied to trees, beaten with sticks and starved for three to four days. On one occasion three or four men were shot for disobedience.'[33]

At the coolie hospital of Dai Ni, just **1** mile from Kanchanaburi and close to the POW camp, where approximately **1,200** *rŏmusha* were accommodated in **12** attap huts, the average daily death count was between **20** and **30** from October 1942 to March 1943.[34]

The conditions under which the native labourers lived shocked even the POWs who themselves were suffering severe privations: 'We hear of frightful casualties from cholera and other diseases among these people, and of the brutality with which they are treated by the Japanese,' Dr Robert Hardie wrote in his secret diary. 'People who have been near these camps speak with bated breath of the state of affairs – corpses rotting unburied in the jungle, almost complete lack of sanitation, a frightful stench, overcrowding, swarms of flies.'[35]

The cemetery at Tarsao camp. (*AWM 01910.005*)

Chapter 5

Escape

1 Only **1** POW is believed to have successfully escaped from the railway camps – Roy Pagani. Rather than wait until nightfall or carry as many provisions as he could. Pagani simply walked away in the middle of the day in bare feet with nothing but a loincloth round his waist. He believed he could adopt the customs of the locals and live as they lived: 'During my stay in the East, I found that a European would always be detected, no matter how good his disguise, due to the lack of sway in his posterior,' Pagani claimed. 'So, of course, this I had perfected whilst a POW, And I had hardened my feet by never wearing any footwear, as bad feet were the escaper's downfall.'[1] **He had also grown a full beard and looked every inch a native Burmese.**

Pagani formulated two escape plans. The first involved heading **10** miles west to the Bay of Bengal where he would steal a boat and then sail along the Burmese coast to India. If he was unable to find a boat, Pagani's second plan involved walking all the way overland through Burma to India.

On the day of his escape, he had breakfast and attended the morning roll call, or *tenko*, as usual but then reported sick. All those who claimed they were sick were given a bashing and then sent out to work anyway. But this meant he was not included in the count of those in the main work party. Once beyond the view of the camp, instead of following the work party he slipped into the jungle. He would not be missed until the evening *tenko* and the Japanese would not be able to start looking for him until daybreak the following morning.

Pagani reached the coast in four hours but failed to find a boat. So, he decided to adopt his alternative plan of walking all the way to India – around **1,000** miles away.

He retraced his steps back to the railway, following the track as far as Thanbyuzayat, and from there across the Salween

River and off into the jungle. After two more days he came to a plantation and, surmising that the owners had prospered under British rule, risked knocking on the door of the main house. As luck would have it the house was the home of a wealthy timber merchant who spoke perfect English and who offered to help the fugitive reach Allied lines.

The merchant proved as good as his word and Pagani was introduced to Major Hugh Seagrim, a 33-year-old British officer in the Karen hills who had joined Force 136, the Far Eastern arm of SOE, tasked with training the loyal Karens to fight the Japanese. The 6 feet 4 inches tall Major Seagrim was called 'Grandfather Longlegs' by the Karens.

Seagrim was delighted to have Pagani join his band, and he placed him in charge of his southern area of operations. The escaped prisoner had become a guerilla leader!

It was perhaps inevitable that eventually his luck would give out. While attempting to cross the River Irrawaddy he was swept away by the current. He was rescued by two Burmese fishermen. Knowing that the Japanese offered a reward for any captured Allied soldiers or airmen, they tried to tie him up but he managed to break free. As he ran away, he was shot.

The wounded escaper was taken to a Japanese guard post and then to hospital. He claimed to be a shot-down American airman, and he was not returned to the railway where he would unquestionably have been executed. He was, though, interrogated and tortured by the dreaded Japanese military police, the *Kempeitai*. But he stuck to his story, and he was sent to Rangoon Docks where he worked for the remainder of the war. Roy Pagani was awarded the Military Medal.[2]

Most camps were without a perimeter fence, hundreds of miles of virtually impenetrable jungle and mountains being a far greater obstacle than any fence could be. In places the jungle was so dense that prisoners of one camp were often unaware that another camp lay only a few hundred metres away. Despite the obvious improbability of making a successful escape, and in the knowledge that failure and recapture would most likely lead to torture and death, some prisoners still left their camps. Lieutenant Colonel F. J. Dillion of 'F' Force explained this phenomenon: 'Several men, sometimes alone, sometimes in groups, disappeared into the jungle. Some probably had the idea of escaping, some undoubtedly only left so as to die in freedom, rather than in captivity, or disease or illness, also ill treatment. The men, on the whole, were in despair. The choice in front of them seemed to be death from disease, or never-ending toil and brutal treatment at the hands of the engineers.'[3]

In December 1942, **4** men escaped through the flimsy bamboo fence at Chungkai camp but, inevitably, they were caught. Later they were taken into the jungle and made to dig their own graves before being shot. About six weeks after this incident, Corporal Alfred Stoten of the Sherwood Foresters was permitted to go into the jungle to attend to the graves. 'There were four separate graves,' he later wrote, 'and at the end of each grave there was a bamboo pole which had been broken off about a foot from the ground. I concluded that these four men had been shot whilst tied to these poles and, after they had been killed, the poles had been broken and the men put into the graves.'[4]

Many of the escape attempts were not well thought out. Two prisoners who escaped from Kanchanaburi camp were captured when they walked into another camp, Tarsau by mistake.[5]

It was the same with **2** British soldiers who tried to escape from Kinsayok camp but were caught at another camp about **20** kilometres away. They were beaten every day for two weeks

A view of the valley of the Khwae Noi, showing just how dense the jungle was and how great a deterrent it was to any escape attempts.

by the Japanese using bamboo, rifles, shovels and fists. Finally, they were taken into the jungle where they were shot.[6]

In the middle of July 1942, **3** men escaped from Bam Pong camp, being among the first to attempt to do so. They slipped out of the camp one night with a supply of food and little else. With no real idea what they were doing they 'floundered around' in the jungle in the night and the following day before they realised they were getting nowhere and gave themselves up to some Thais who handed the prisoners to the Japanese.

Though they were not executed, they were made to stand to attention outside the camp's guardroom for several days before being taken to Singapore and handed long prison sentences. **2** of them survived to make the journey home at the end of the war.

The escape attempt prompted the Japanese camp commander to insist that the senior POW officer, Lieutenant Colonel Williamson, sign a paper declaring that he would not escape and that he would prevent any of the prisoners whom he commanded from escaping. Williamson refused, upon which he was told he would be shot. Williamson remained defiant and the threatened shooting did not occur.[7]

Nevertheless, the escape attempt led to Lieutenant Colonel Nagatoma, commander of No. 3 Branch Thailand POW Administration, to demand that 'war prisoners' must sign a declaration which read: 'I the undersigned hereby solemnly swear on my honour that I will not under any circumstances attempt escape'.

Nagatoma made it clear that those who refused to sign such a declaration would be 'locked in'. That is exactly what happened to Major Green at Kandaw camp after he refused to sign the document. On 5 October 1942 he was taken to Thanbyuzayat base camp and placed in close confinement. This was: 'a plain cell, very dark, hard uneven floor,' observed Brigadier Varley the most senior Allied officer in the camps. 'Not allowed anything to lie [on] or take anything in with him. Not even lavatory paper. These later duties were carried out in a corner of the room through a trap door, excreta etc., depositing under floorboards. No water allowed for washing of body or hands. Food plain rice with salt sprinkled over it, making it unpalatable. Plain water to drink 3 times daily, sometimes weak tea. No blanket, bag or anything to lie on or rest head.'

Green was not alone in refusing to sign the declaration and Brigadier Varley had to explain to Nagatoma that it was every British and Australian soldier's duty to try and escape. Eventually, after Varley had made it clear that signing any such declaration under compulsion rendered it invalid, the prisoners complied. Consequently, the escapes continued.

On the Burmese side of the railway there were **13** escape attempts by the end of November 1942. This included the sad case of Private G. H. Whitefield. On 10 November 1942, Whitefield slipped out of Kendaw camp. He soon gave himself up, however, because he said that the natives, who were offered **100** rupees by the Japanese for each man they captured, knew of his whereabouts and movements. According to his commanding officer, Whitefield had always behaved erratically, and a hastily assembled medical board declared he was 'Physically sound, but slightly deficient mentally, and a moral imbecile, not responsible for his actions'. Lieutenant Naito interviewed Whitefield himself and he agreed that the man was unbalanced and declared he would not be punished. That seemed to be the end of the matter until 14 December when he was taken to the camp cemetery and shot.

On 8 October four Dutch, on 21 November three Dutch, and four days later a further four Dutch soldiers also tried to escape from the Burmese camps. All these Dutch escapees were Eurasians. It would seem that of the last group one of the Dutch prisoners was shot when surrounded by Burmese and three others were seized and handed back to the Japanese.

At Nong Pladuk camp, a slightly different approach was taken by the Japanese. The senior POW officer, Major W. E. Gill, and his second in charge, Major Sykes, were told by Lieutenant Colonel Sasaki that they would 'have their heads cut off' if any prisoners attempted to escape.

In February 1943, a group of **3** men from Thetkaw camp made a carefully planned and determined attempt to reach India. They were Major A. Mull, Sapper A.J. Bell and Gunner K. J. Dickinson. The group reached a few miles north of Moulmein when Dickinson fell out, exhausted. As had been agreed, the others went on. Dickinson was recaptured by the Japanese, taken to Thanbyuzayat, and executed without trial. Mull and Bell went on and had reached **100** miles farther north when they encountered a pro-Japanese native patrol. Mull was killed in the struggle and Bell was badly wounded. He was taken to Thanbyuzayat and he too was executed.[8]

Bell's conduct at his execution was described as exemplary. 'He thanked Lieutenant Naito, who was in charge of the firing squad, for his courtesy and for the privileges extended to him. He shook hands, refused to kneel or sit in a tied position as was the Japanese custom, stating that he would die on his feet.'[9]

10

The largest recorded mass escape attempt involved **10** men from Songkurai camp on 5 July 1943. Lieutenant J. B. Bradley RE, Lieutenant Colonel Wilkinson RE, captains W. H. Anker, RASC, J. Feathers, RASC, lieutenants Robinson, RASC, I. M. Moffat, RE, G. A. Machade, SSVF, T.P.D. Jones, Malay Regiment, Corporal Brown, SSVF, and Nur Mohammed, an Indian fisherman who had been taken prisoner by the Japanese, slipped out of the camp with the aim of walking through the mountainous jungles to reach the Ye River. They planned to raft down the river until they reached the coast of Burma.

One of the escapees, Colonel Wilkinson, was a very experienced yachtsmen and Lieutenant Bradley had also sailed small boats so when they reached the Burmese coast they would, by whatever means, acquire a yacht and sail across the Andaman Sea to freedom.

In preparation for the journey they were to undertake, the prisoners sold everything of value they possessed so that they had ready cash with which they could buy food or pay locals to help them. They also managed to accumulate **70** pounds of rice, and some soya beans, dried fish, whitebait, chillies and a few tins of canned fish. In addition, they had some quinine tablets and water purifying tablets plus some candles and matches as well as mugs and billycans and a couple of compasses.[10]

One of the officers left a note explaining why they had sought to escape: 'Food is short, health is failing, sickness such as

Beriberi, Cholera, Malaria, Small Pox, Dysentery and Diphtheria is prevalent. Some 220 officers and men have died since our arrival here about five weeks ago ...therefore, I consider, with some of my fellow companions, that the risk we are about to take, be it life or death, is to some purpose if only to get away from here.'[11]

James Bradley, who wrote an account of the escape attempt, echoed those sentiments. He fully accepted that he was likely to die of starvation in the jungle or at the hands of the Japanese if caught, but that his chances of survival in the work camps were equally slim.

The **10** men soon ran into problems. The stream they had hoped to walk up to hide their tracks had turned into a raging torrent. They desperately needed to conceal the direction they had taken and so had no choice but to wade up the stream against the rushing water. Eventually, they felt they had moved far enough away from the camp to risk striking out overland from the stream.

For the first few days they made reasonable progress through light jungle. They ate morning and evening, creating a makeshift bamboo shelter each night, lighting a fire to cook their food and to keep away the tigers which were known to inhabit the region.

On 18 July it was noticed that Lieutenant Robinson's hand, which had become poisoned had become badly festered. At this point they also reached mountainous terrain and the dense jungle on the slopes of the mountains became so thick that progress was pitifully slow – the group managing to climb just half a kilometre a day.

Their rations dwindled until, on 25 July, they ate the last of their rice and **3** days later shared **1** small tin of pilchards between all **10** men. During the night Corporal Brown, riddled with tropical ulcers, walked out into the jungle to die, not wanting to be a burden upon the rest. Others developed injuries from hacking their way through the undergrowth and Lieutenant Moffat's legs had become covered in tropical ulcers. On 2 August, Captain Feathers died during the night and three days later Colonel Wilkinson died from heart failure. On 9 August Lieutenant Jones collapsed unconscious and had to be carried to a hut next to a tributary of the Ye. In the hut Lieutenant Robinson died from septicaemia and dysentery, and the same night Jones begged them to carry on without him as he was virtually unable to move.

On 14 August, after **6** weeks, the last **2** of which were without food, the survivors reached the Ye and built a raft. This took **3** days, and on 17 August they set off down the river. They did not get far before the raft broke up in rapids. Three managed to reach the shore where they were found by Burmese hunters – who gave the escapees the first food they had had in **20** days. They were taken to the native village where they appeared to be warmly welcomed. But they noticed that they were continually being watched, and they suspected that their presence had been reported to the local authorities. Indeed, the next day saw the arrival of two Japanese soldiers accompanied by a Burmese police inspector and three policemen.

The escapees were in no state to resist and they were taken initially to Japanese Headquarters at Ye and transferred into the hands of the *Kempeitai* (described by Ken Adams as 'stocky little policemen with a fondness for torture, dark glasses and swords that were too big for them,'[12]) who took them to Moulmein and eventually Thanbyuzayat where they were placed in a small, leaky hut. 'We had just enough room for the four of us to lie

A punishment hole in one of the camps. POWs captured after attempting to escape often found themselves placed in such cages before facing the ultimate penalty – execution. (*AWM 157872*)

down,' related James Bradley. 'Every night we were handcuffed together.' They were told Thanbyuzayat was where they would be executed. A number of POWs who were recovering from cholera were ordered to cut bamboo for the pyre upon which the bodies of the escapees would be burned.

They were repeatedly interrogated and beaten and the only food they were given was a ball of rice each twice a day along with a little water. However, in almost unique circumstances, thanks to the efforts of the British and Australian officers, the Japanese were persuaded to drop the death sentences, and the men went back to work on the railway.

Others were not so fortunate. A group of **8** escaped undetected from Chungkai camp at dawn on 6 July 1943. They had a small compass and a map which had been hidden from the Japanese plus they took with them quantities of rice, beans and dried fish they had stolen from the Japanese storeroom.

At first, they made good progress, even digging up root vegetables and picking mangoes and other fruit from an abandoned village. They even received help from the villagers at one *kampong* who directed them to a cave where they could safely hide until the dry season as further progress in the height of the monsoon was impracticable. Not far from the cave they found more fruit and vegetables from another abandoned village. But it was at this time that one of them died from either dengue fever or malaria. Some of the villagers who had directed them the cave also showed them how to catch fish by torchlight at night.

Their presence became known to too many locals and eventually they were sold out to the Japanese, though only **4** of the escapees were in the cave at the time of their capture.[13]

Details of the escape and recapture were recorded in the following translation of 'Japanese Court Martial Case and Summary of Evidence' selected from a file of Court Martial Records belonging to the Legal Department of 18 Area Army:[14]

Accused:
Ian O'Brian Poston Bradley, British Army Sgt
Peter Richard Jackson, British Army Sgt
Bernard Bradley, British Army, L/Cpl

Frederick John 'Urado', British Other Rank
Jack Ivor Evans, British Army Cpl
William Henry Dawkins, British Army L/Cpl

Unit:	2 Detached Station, 4 Section, Malay PW Camp
Offence:	Acts contrary to PW Camp Penal Laws
Sentence:	Penal Servitude for Life
Date of Sentence:	18 November 1943

The accused were captured in Singapore and were sent to 2 Detached Station for work on the Burma-Siam Railway. There was an outbreak of Cholera in early June 1943 and the accused felt unhappy and longed to return home.

Among the PWs was a man called Medley who had been in Siam before and knew the language and topography. On 5 June the accused got together and planned to escape to China or India and so return home. The accused men and another PW called Singleton sold various articles through Medley to Siamese who were working on the railway, and also got some food from the PW in charge of the cookhouse. Bradley got a lodestone from another PW and four maps were made.

Preparations for the escape were then complete, and on 6 June the accused and Singleton escaped under Medley's guidance (a total of 8 men).

In the middle of July, the party had reached a cave in the jungle near 'Chiyenaboe', 12 Km East of 'Nonaipon' (Siam) but it was the rainy season and free movement was impossible.

During their concealment, Singleton died on 13 September. On 2 October Evans, Dawkins and Medley went out to buy food and the other four were captured by the Kempeitai. Medley continued to do his utmost to escape but, on 7 October Evans and Dawkins gave themselves up to Japanese officials of the Mitsubishi Mining Co. at 'Daibu' and they were handed over to the Moulmein Kempei on 14 October.

Signed:
Lt Col Shitamura Chikara, President of the Court
Lt Ishihashi Tsuki, Court Member
Lt Koyama Mayata, Court Member

Lance Corporal Bernard Bradley died in Outram Road Jail, but the others survived to the end of the war.

In March 1943, **4** POWs escaped from Tha Kilen camp and a huge hunt was undertaken by heavily armed *Kempeitai* as well as Thais eager for the handsome reward on offer for the capture of the prisoners. Sergeants Francis Kelly and Edward Reay along with Fusilier Timothy Kenneally and Private Patrick Fitzgerald broke out of the camp with the aim of reaching the Burmese coast at Maungmagan, some **60** miles from Tha Kilen.

Their absence was covered up by the other prisoners during *tenko* with men moving around as they made 'urgent' visits to the latrine. This deception was maintained for a couple of days before the commanding officer had to announce that four of his men were missing. They were caught just **16** miles away near the Burmese border. Fitzgerald was shot during capture and the others were later executed at Khao Pun, without trial, on 23 March 1943.

Lieutenant Christopher Raymond of the 3rd Indian Corps Signals saw the graves in the jungle two or three days after the execution. He saw the 'rough graves and bamboo frames in the shape of a cross. It looked as though some persons had been tied to them, they were marked, and there were some stains which looked like blood stains ... They were about three-quarters of a mile from the camp in a little clearing in the jungle. There were no names on them.' Major General Sasa, who ordered the executions, met a similar fate after being found guilty of war crimes in 1946.

In another incident at Tarsao camp, a very ill and weak soldier of the Sherwood Foresters was accused of attempting to escape. The prisoners were lined up to observe what happened to escapees who were caught. The unfortunate Forester was tied to the front of a locomotive on the orders of the camp commandant, Lieutenant Sugano: 'at Sugano's signal to the engine driver, exhaust steam gushed from the locomotive's cylinders,' recalled Bill Reed of 252 Battery, 63 Anti-Tank Regiment, Oxfordshire Yeomanry, 'and it moved slowly forward with its living human buffers and commenced shunting work in the sidings.'[15]

At Tamarkan camp, **2** officers and **4** other ranks escaped on 28 January 1943. The camp commander, Lieutenant Colonel

Toosey, was able to conceal the escapers absence from the Japanese roll calls for two days. After ten days the **4** other ranks were captured and returned under armed escort to the camp where they were locked up in the Guard Room. Two days later they were driven into the jungle and never seen again. Reports of shots being fired were received from locals. On 20 February the **2** officers, Captain E.C. Pomeroy and Lieutenant Howard, were also brought back into the camp. On 23 February these **2** were also driven into the jungle where, again according to the Thais, they were bayonetted to death.[16]

Even being suspected of attempting to escape could have fatal consequences. At Hindaine camp **2** Dutch prisoners were alleged to have attempted to escape. Yet the camp was deep in the jungle, and it was felt there was no need for a perimeter fence as there was nowhere for the prisoners to escape to. This meant that there was no marked boundary around Hindaine and the two men were seen beyond what the Japanese determined were the confines of the camp. Despite their protests of innocence, they were sentenced to death. What happened to them was witnessed by Lance Corporal A. Prime of the Royal Corps of Signals. One of the prisoners was beheaded with a sword and the other Dutch soldier, having witnessed the beheading, 'ran amok and was bayonetted'.[17]

There was also the strange case of Sergeant Ron O'Donnell who was allegedly shot for trying to escape in somewhat peculiar circumstances. He had been taken into the jungle from Hlepauk camp by one of the Japanese guards called Tomoto, but only the latter returned. When O'Donnell's body was returned to camp, it was seen that he had suffered injuries to his head and been shot in the chest at close range which did not correspond with someone trying to run away. The prisoners believed that Tomoto had a sexual interest in O'Donnell who rebuffed the guard's advances. The camp commander, Corporal Tanaka, chose to accept Tomoto's version of events.[18]

The truth was that, Roy Pagani apart, there was no realistic chance of escaping as Lieutenant John Durford had, painfully, to accept. He and **6** other officers at Tonchan camp formed an 'escape committee'. With what information the officers had,

Even if escaping prisoners managed to cut their way through the dense jungle they then had to overcome the barrier of the mountains.

they concluded that the only way for them to escape would be to trek through the jungle to the ports on the Andaman Sea where they hoped to bribe a local Thai to take them to safety. One day Durnford undertook a solo reconnaissance to gauge the practicality of their plan. He sneaked out of camp and climbed **1,000** feet to the top of a hill behind the railway clearing. He saw in every direction endless jungle-clad, rock-tipped, mountains. He knew then that the terrain held the prisoners captive more effectively than any barbed-wire fence or machine-gun post ever could.

Chapter 6

Construction and Completion

1 The very last spike was ceremoniously hammered into the final sleeper on 17 October 1943 as the two ends of the railway met at Konkuita to mark the completion of the railway. There are a number of slightly differing accounts of this ceremony, one of which states that the commanders of the two railway regiments – Colonel Sasaki of the 5th Railway Regiment and Colonel Imai of the 9th – each drove a golden spike into the final sleeper (these were later removed and replaced with the standard iron ones[1]).

Then, a Japanese C-5631 steam locomotive from the Thailand side, decorated with crossed Rising Sun flags, pulled **10** wagons across the joining point into Burma, followed by a Burmese type KS locomotive which did the same from the Burma side.

A commemorative service was then held during which General Iashida addressed the gathering: 'In the hard construction work we lost ...1,000 Japanese soldiers, 12,000 prisoners of war, 8,400 workers from Burma, Thailand and Malaya. May their souls rest in peace.'[2]

Another account described a more elaborate event which was the subject of a Japanese propaganda film, showing the

The iconic symbol of the Thailand-Burma railway, the bridge at Kanchanaburi.

laying of the last section of track and the hammering home of the final spike. For the film, the producers needed fit-looking healthy prisoners happily working for the Emperor. A few, a little less skeletal than others, were selected and handed nice Japanese shirts, shorts and shoes.

The bridge is still in use, with three trains a day each way crossing its **300**-metre length. One of the many bombs aimed at the bridge sits still unexploded.

After a rehearsal, the camera began to roll, and the prisoners laid the last section of track and began driving home the spikes. One of the prisoners recorded what happened next: 'As the last spike was ready to be driven a most important but self-conscious looking senior and overweight officer of the Japanese Army came forward to perform the symbolic driving of the last spike. Panting with the weight of the hammer this portly dignitary aimed a feeble blow at the head of the spike which he missed completely and gave the rail a resounding clang instead. Bracing himself and looking quite dismayed at his own clumsiness, the officer took a much shorter grip of the hammer and managed to drive the spike in a fraction into the sleeper to be finished off by a lithe engineer who leaped to his assistance.' Needless to say, the prisoners were made to return their new clothes and shoes.[3] After the railway had been finished, most of the work camps were abandoned and the prisoners moved to a small number of base camps.

31 is how many spur tracks branched off from the main line into the jungle. Mostly, their length was **500** metres. They were adopted for daytime protection from Allied air attacks.

688 was the number of trestle bridges built along the railway, including between **6** and **8** long-span bridges. In total, the bridges stretched for a distance of **14** kilometres.[4] One of the best-known bridges

The Wampo viaduct, then and now. The ledge upon which the track was laid was cut from the top of the rock face downwards. Remarkably, this took just **17** days, but it involved the labour of around **2,000** men.

was called the 'pack of cards' bridge by the prisoners because it collapsed **3** times during its period of construction. The bridge was **400** yards long and **80** feet high. It was built of timber fastened with wooden wedges and dowels, spikes, and rattan ropes. It is known that **31** prisoners were killed in falls from the bridge during construction and a further **29** were beaten to death.[5] Ultimately it was abandoned in favour of an embankment which led up to 'Compressor Cutting'.

During the dry season less than **20** per cent of the bridges crossed 'wet' gaps. All the others were ravines or flood openings. During the monsoon, all of those became raging torrents and, as

The Three Tier Bridge then and all that remains now is its foundations.

can be seen on photographs, all the wooden bridges were built with short spans which increased the danger of heavy objects washed downstream crashing against the supporting piles. To lessen this danger, the piles were often tied together in bundles. This proved particularly effective when bombs were dropped near bridges as often only the outer piles would be damaged.[6]

There was also the danger of these wooden bridges catching fire during the dry season from the surrounding jungle. Consequently, the majority of the bridges had a permanent guard, and the risk of fire was reduced by the placing of bamboo matting with an earth covering at both ends of each bridge.

8 All but **8** of these **688** bridges were made entirely of locally-cut timber. This wood was not the renowned Siamese teak but was softwood. The hardwood teak was used to power the steam locomotives as its higher density produced more heat, and, as we have read, for sleepers. Although the Japanese knew that the softwood would need to be replaced at least every **3** years, it was much easier to cut and to bolt together, especially as they lacked mechanical equipment. This was particularly important when the railway was bombed as it was far quicker and easier to repair using softwood.

At Tha Kilen, **98** kilometres from Bam Pong, a spur line branches off to the POW camp and the Khwae Noi river.

2

Of all these bridges, there were only **2** that crossed the Khwae Noi. These were the wooden bridges of Onte and Fukushima. Both of these were built entirely by Japanese engineers. All the other bridges spanned the river's tributaries.[7] In total, the prisoners and *rǒmusha* hauled **60,000** cubic metres of bridging timber poles.[8]

2,000

The gradient of the railway increased as it was carried over the Tenasserim Hills which run along the Burma/Thailand border, reaching a height of approximately **2,000** feet above sea level. The steepest gradient along the line was on the approach to the Three Pagodas Pass. This was a rise of **27.5** metres in **1,000** metres. Usually, two locomotives were used to get the trains up this stretch of track, one pushing and one pulling.

7

was the average distance in kilometres between passing loops. Being a single track railway, the loops were the means by which traffic could run up and down the line simultaneously. The loops were, on average, between **350** and **450** metres long, though some were shorter and were, in many cases sited near stations. At

The Three Pagodas Pass marked the border between Thailand and Burma, or what is today Myanmar.

A true 'then and now' photograph of the Three Pagodas Pass as it was in 1945. (*AWM P01910.025*)

57 of those stations (roughly every **20** kilometres along the track) were facilities, such as water for the steam engines. These water facilities usually consisted of engine-driven pumps which pumped the water from a well or from the river into an elevated tank.

Remains of the track still lead up towards the Myanmar border.

A telegraph line ran alongside the railway, composed of **2** or more pairs of wires. One of these was of **200** pounds copper, the other **200** pounds galvanised iron.[9]

The stations were generally the same, with long platforms with the station buildings placed in the adjacent jungle. All the important stations had well-camouflaged sidings for loading and unloading and to conceal them from the air. Often, the only buildings which could be detected by aircraft were those of the associated POW and *rǒmusha* camps. These buildings included so-called 'staging stations' for Japanese troops, especially officers, which were *hectans*, or hotels, to accommodate the troops if they were held up by attacks by Allied aircraft or other unforeseen events.

Lieutenant Colonel E. E. Dunlop, Commanding Officer 2/2nd Casualty Clearing Station (right), and Lieutenant Colonel A. E. Coates, Chief Medical Officer, Nakon Paton Prisoner of War Hospital (left). (*AWM 117362*)

890

During the **15** months of the construction period an average of **890** metres of track was laid per day.[10]

2,300

As the railway was nearing completion, from September 1943 those prisoners no longer engaged on the line were sent back to base camps and hospitals. One of these was at Kanchanaburi where food was more plentiful and the fit men were issued with footwear and clothing. Sickness levels rapidly dropped, though hospital accommodation there was hopelessly inadequate, with **2,300** patients crowded into an area **750** feet wide by **1,850** feet long.[11]

Restrictions on many activities were also relaxed after the railway had been finished, with almost idyllic scenes playing out in camps that had previously seen unspeakable horrors, as Len Gibson described: 'Some men managed to acquire some fat or oil and with a piece of string to serve as a wick made a crude lamp using an empty can. By this poor light men would play cards; often with home-made ones. Others would light fires and sit out in the open. I often took out my guitar and played at the camp fires and if Charley Carney and Michael Conlin joined in it would develop into a concert.'[12]

17,110

was the number of surviving POWs who were sent back to Singapore after the completion of the railway, and **10,770** of these were shipped to Japan and Formosa to continue to work on projects for the Japanese. According to the official

Japanese report, **1,000** 'healthy prisoners' undertook 'urgent and indispensable supplementary construction work related to the railway, the rest being left with lessened labour'. That lessened labour for those who remained in the camps took the form of maintenance and repair work on the railway, which continued until the Japanese surrender. [13]

In addition to those POWs, around **9,000** Japanese remained on the railway, who were aided by about **22,000** Asian labourers.

The Japanese 5th Railway Regiment was also redeployed once the railway was up and running, being transferred to operations in central Burma.

1.5

was the cost in millions of Japanese yen of the building of Nakom Paton hospital which was established by the Japanese in December 1943 to handle chronic and heavy sick patients. It was located on the main Singapore-Thailand railway, **56** kilometres west of Bangkok. The hospital was built to accommodate **10,000** beds.

It came about following discussions on what to do with the POWs after the completion of the railway. The supposed 'light' sick were to be placed in the hospital base camps and those considered very ill were to go to the new Nakom Paton hospital.

By January 1944, **50** large huts for up to **200** men each had been built, and separate medical huts had been constructed. Within three months the camp was all but full, with **8,000-10,000** patients.

In the summer of 1944, a new Japanese medical officer was appointed to Nakom Paton named Lieutenant Siguchi, who immediately began to move patients out of the hospital by declaring

The Hintok Tampi bridge showing the metre-wide track. Just visible in the background is the start of Hellfire Pass.

them fit for work. He refused to consider a person unfit for work unless he had some gross abnormality such as tropical ulcers or amputations. A patient suffering from malaria or dysentery was not regarded by Siguchi as being ill. As a result, large numbers of men were transferred back to the railway base camps.

25

In January 1945 when the number of men available for working at Nakom Paton was practically nil, Siguchi conducted a tour of the wards and practically every man who could stand was sent out on a working party about **1,000** strong – it was referred to by Alfred Coats as a 'Death March'. These men were sent to southern Thailand to build a road between Prachuab Kirikun and Mergui – universally known as the Mergui Road. It was cut through virgin jungle, working hours were long and conditions as bad as at any time during the construction of the railway.

Albert Raven described arriving at the work camp: 'It was more foul and primitive than any camp I had ever seen. Its mud floors were littered with filth and a horrible stench permeated the atmosphere. A feeling of fear and foreboding gripped me. Both ahead and behind us lay the dense jungle. No further supplies of food would reach us until the road was through from the base at Kirikan and we would never leave this camp until we had flung the road over the mountains towards Mergui. We were trapped high above the world in this seemingly impenetrable jungle and the only means of exit rested entirely on the efforts that could be extracted from our weak and weary bodies.'[14]

Bullock carts were used on the road, with **2** bullocks being used to pull a cart containing **6** large bags of rice. When bullocks died the Japanese replaced them with POWs, and **6** men were employed to haul **10** bags.[15]

Six weeks later **230,** or practically **25** per cent, had died.[16]

Chapter 7

Running the Railway

35,552

Apart from the few POWs who were kept for maintenance work after the completion of the line, the running of the railway was in the hands of the Japanese and the Asiatics. All the administrative work was undertaken by the Japanese and some Malays, Indians and Javanese. The drivers were largely Javanese and Malays. The workshop technicians were predominately Japanese from railway workshops in Japan with support from Chinese, Javanese and Malays. In total, this amounted to **35,552** men. It is said these men 'volunteered' for these jobs but that was only after the Japanese had dismissed them from their civilian jobs, offering them work in Thailand and Burma instead. Nevertheless, they were treated quite well and saw themselves far superior to the coolies. They received food and accommodation for free with part of their salaries being sent back to their families. They were also allowed to send and receive letters.

An aerial reconnaissance photograph of the bridges over the Mae Klong River at Kanchanaburi taken on 19 April 1944.

A trainload of *rŏmusha* on their way home in October 1945. (*AWM 120502*)

With the completion of the railway, the prisoners were moved back to base camps, some being taken by train as these troops were in early 1943. (*AWM P00406.011*)

As well as the workshops at Kanchanaburi, there were also ones established at Wampo, Kinsayok, Brankasi, Nike, Apalon, and Thanbyuzayat. These had 'ample' facilities for the upgrade and repair of locomotives and the upkeep of wagons.

On the Thailand side the running of the railway was taken over by 4th Special Organised Civilian Railway Force. This was chiefly composed of civilian railway men originally exempted from military service who were eventually drafted. They received only elementary military training.[1]

2

There were no fixed signal stations along the line, all signalling being performed by the station masters with **2** flags. As a train approached each station, the station master would stand on the platform with a red flag and a green flag. 'He shows red when the train has to stop at a certain point of his station,' explained a post-war report. 'If he shows green, then the train stops too, but may pass the flag. Even if the train driver has been notified by a previous station that he has to stop, either of the flags must still be shown. If a train may pass the station without stopping the station master makes a circular move with the green flag. Showing both flags above the shoulders (arms crossed) means: drive slowly.'[2]

20 The early construction at either end of the railway was done reasonably well as this work was carried out before the 'speedo' period. Cuttings were wide, and the roadbed was sound. As construction progressed, and pushed through at a greater rate, this standard noticeably deteriorated; cuttings became so narrow as to barely permit a train to pass through, and other faults, in consequence, developed: e.g., sleepers sank flush into the formation, collapses occurred, and there were landslides in cuttings. Bridges which, at their best, were only meant to be temporary, were soon in very bad state, particularly on the Burma side. As a result, the Burma side of the line was closed in June 1946. This meant that the railway only operated in full for **20** months.

45 was the number of locomotives shipped from Japan to run on the railway. There were also **30** from Malaya, **25** from Borneo, **4** from Thailand and **9** from Java, making a total of **113**. By the end of the war around **100** of the original engines were still in operation.[3] Engines from Malaya and Burma were wood-burning and less powerful than the coal-burning Japanese locomotives, but they were easier to supply as they could be fuelled from wood

One of the locomotives used on the railway has been preserved and is on display at Kanchanaburi.

One of the engines on display was built in Scotland and was most likely shipped from Malaya.

cut locally. These trains were allocated to the gentler sections of the railway. They would pass their rolling stock onto more powerful trains when the railway reached the hills running up to the Three Pagodas Pass.

For this, the prisoners had to cut down teak trees on a 'job and finish' basis. Divided into teams of **6**, the men had to fell the trees and then cut them into logs averaging **18** inches long. Each team was expected to produce **6** cubic metres of wood per day. This was later increased first to **6.5** metres a day and then to **7**.[4]

Of the rolling stock and wagons, **400** came from Japan, **1,000** from Malaya, and **400** from Burma. This was a total of **1,800**.[5]

As well as locomotives, the Japanese introduced **100** diesel motor trucks which were converted to run on the railway track. Called 'Flying Kampongs' by the prisoners, these were primarily

One of the trucks converted to run on railway tracks has been preserved at Kanchanaburi. These were a standard Japanese design, not exclusively for use on the Thailand-Burma railway. Known locally as 'Flying Kampongs', they were capable of pulling four of the kind of trailers seen here.

used for the transportation of maintenance parties or Japanese troops, with **100** or **120** men being carried in the **4** trailers normally pulled by the motors. They could travel at between **35** and **50** kilometres an hour, and were, therefore, given priority over the slower-moving trains. However, they were not designed for long-distance travel and the trucks had to be changed regularly. These were usually fitted with a bamboo and attap roof over both the truck and the trailers. This served both as shade for those being transported along the line and as camouflage to conceal them from Allied aircraft.[6]

20 was about how many wagons were pulled by each locomotive. Generally, there were water pumps at each station and an accommodation hut for repair gangs. One unidentified person (known only as 'M-97') undertook the journey from Bam Pong to Thanbyuzayat in the first week of March 1944. 'The single line was in a very bad condition and travel was extremely precarious owing to bad foundations. The Siam section of the railway, up to the border, was in a very bad state of repair. Bridges were down at several points and the rails damaged.' M-97 noticed derailed and abandoned vans and at one point the vans, or wagons, had fallen several hundred feet down a deep gorge.[7]

The track had been so poorly made and had been the subject of sabotage whenever the opportunity fell to the prisoners, that sleepers sank flush with the ground and there were landslides in the cuttings.

Generally, the load of each train was made up of from **2** to **5** carloads of ammunition (always in the centre of the train), ordnance stores, supplies etc (in the forward part) and petrol stores (in the rear). The 9th Railway Regiment gives the distribution for the total period December 1943–August 1945, as follows:

Ordnance Stores	**28,050** tons
Ammunition	**68,900** tons
Clothing	**6,800** tons
Provisions	**60,000** tons
Petrol	**53,020** tons
Oils, Lubricants	**2,780** tons
Miscellaneous	**10,000** tons

POWs loading petrol and stores onto a 'Flying Kampong' in 1943. (*AWM P00406.061*)

10 tons was the maximum axle load. This was calculated from the weight of the heaviest of the locomotives to be used on the railway, the C56 type. A rail of **60–75** pounds per metre could bear as much as **13–17** tons, but the weak structure of the railway meant that such high levels could not be risked.

Wanglan, or Wang Lan, station is still in use today.

was the highest number of trains which ran per day during the operation of the railway from its completion until the end of the war. According to records of the Japanese 9th Railway Regiment, in December 1944, **115** trains carried supplies from Thailand to Burma. In January 1945, as a result of damage to the railway from air attacks and the deteriorating condition of the track, the number dropped to **60**.

The figures below show the number in two-month periods:

1943	Dec–Jan	**1–2** trains per day
1944	Feb–Apr	**2** trains per day
	May–Jun	**2–3** trains per day
	Jul–Aug	**3–4** trains per day
	Sept–Oct	**4** trains per day
	Nov-Dec	**5** trains per day
1945	Jan–Feb	**2** trains per day
	Mar–Apr	**2–3** trains per day
	Jun–Jul	**2** trains per day

One factor which caused problems for the railway officials was that the Japanese stock had a different coupling system and was at a different height to that of the Malay-Thai stock. This meant that the trains had to be composed of all Japanese stock or all Malay-Thai stock. Just to make matters worse, the Javanese stock had yet another different coupling system.

The Japanese 9th Railway Regiment compiled figures showing volume of supplies moved into Burma by months giving the distribution by commodities:

Year/Month	*Trains per month*	*Per train wagons*	*Tonnage ordnance*	*Transported ammunition*	*P.O.L.*	*Misc.*
1943						
Nov	**45**	**20**	**2,800**	**3,000**		**1,800**
Dec	**50**	**20**	**2,500**	**4,200**		**2,800**
1944						
Jan	**60**	**20**	**2,400**	**4,500**		**4,500**
Feb	**65**	**20**	**2,000**	**4,500**	**1,500**	**4,350**

Year/Month	*Trains per month*	*Per train wagons*	*Tonnage ordnance*	*Transported ammunition*	*P.O.L.*	*Misc.*
Mar	**65**	**20**	**2,150**	**4,500**	**1,200**	**4,500**
Apr	**70**	**20**	**1,150**	**3,500**	**1,500**	**4,000**
May	**75**	**20**	**1,250**	**4,000**	**3,000**	**3,000**
Jun	**80**	**20**	**1,000**	**4,000**	**5,700**	**2,000**
Jul	**85**	**20**	**2,500**	**4,500**	**5,700**	**2,950**
Aug	**90**	**20**	**2,000**	**4,500**	**5,700**	**4,900**
Sept	**95**	**20**	**550**	**5,500**	**6,000**	**6,000**
Oct	**100**	**20**	**1,000**	**5,500**	**6,000**	**7,000**
Nov	**110**	**20**	**2,400**	**5,000**	**6,000**	**7,000**
Dec	**115**	**20**	**2,850**	**5,000**	**7,000**	**7,000**
1945						
Jan	**60**	**20**	**400**	**3,500**	**3,500**	**4,000**
Feb	**65**	**20**	**500**	**1,200**	**1,000**	**2,500**
Mar	**70**	**20**	**500**	**1,000**	**1,000**	**2,800**
Apr	**70**	**20**	**400**	**500**	**500**	**2,500**
May	**75**	**20**	**200**	**1,000**		
Jun	**60**	**20**	**1,000**			
Jul	**60**	**20**	**500**			
Aug	**40**	**20**	**200**			

Wang Yen station is also still in use.

The true purpose of the railway was to move troops and equipment into Burma to mount a bid to invade British-held India. During the crucial battles of Imphal and Kohima, it took **6** weeks for reinforcements from Bangkok to reach the front line. Below are the reinforcements which were transferred to Burma from Thailand on the railway:

Period	*Unit*
Dec 1943	Retsu Butai (31st Division)
Feb–Apr 1944	Okami Butai (49th Division)
Mar–Apr 1944	168 Infantry Regiment (49th Division)
May–Jun 1944	Yasu Division (53rd Division)

16

The running of the railway was severely hampered by attacks from Allied aircraft which damaged **16** locomotives by bombing and/or strafing. Of these **11** were damaged beyond repair but the other **5** were put back into service. Also damaged by aerial attacks were **10** passenger coaches, **70** covered wagons, **40** open wagons and **15** flat wagons. Of this total of **135** wagons damaged, **78** were repaired.[8] The failure of the Japanese to run the amount of goods and personnel along the completed railway was largely due to the air raids.

29

was how many POWs were killed outright in the first fatal bombing raid against the railway at Thanbuzayat undertaken by the Strategic Air Force, Eastern Air Command of the Allied Air Force. As the terminus of the Burma end of the railway and a large site with workshops and other facilities, it would clearly be subjected to Allied bombing raids. Well aware of this, Brigadier Varley sought permission to dig slit trenches for the prisoners to shelter in. This was approved – but only after they had dug trenches for the Japanese troops. Varley also received permission to form a red cross on the ground at the hospital out of red soil and sand. When completed, the cross was **70** metres long and **70** metres wide.

That first fatal bombing attack was on 12 June 1943, and though no bombs struck the POW camp, some men were hit in the village at the water pump. According to Brigadier Varley,

An 8 January 1945 photo recce image of the bridges which cross the Winyaw River at Shitpyit near Anankwin (45 Kilo) camp under attack from an RAF Liberator. The lower bridge is the main steel-and-concrete bridge, while the upper bridge is a wooden bypass. Possibly the main bridge was breached before this photo was taken. At lower left are zigzag slit trenches and camp buildings. (*AWM P02491.294*)

during the attack the Japanese 'became very excited, rushing around in all directions shouting, fixing bayonets, and loading rifles, and nobody was allowed outside the huts on penalty of being shot', but there were no POW casualties. Three days later, the bombers returned. The POW camp was surrounded on three sides by Japanese installations, and these were targeted by the Allied bombers. Some Japanese even tried shooting at the aircraft from inside the camp. As a result, the aircraft bombed and machine-gunned the camp. As well as those killed during the raid, a further **70** were wounded of whom **15** later died.[9]

Among those wounded was Varley himself. The day after the second of these raids the Japanese ordered the evacuation of the camp.

Aerial reconnaissance photograph of the damage to the famous bridge over the Mae Klong River bridge by the bombing raid of 24 June 1945. Note the unscathed wooden bridge which was built before the main concrete and steel bridge. (*AWM P00502.001*)

The Allied aircraft continued to attack the railway at every opportunity. Kanchanaburi and its famous bridge was a frequent target. The first raid against the bridge took place on 29 November 1944. This caused some damage but also resulted in the death of some prisoners when one bomb fell in the camp.

The second attack against the bridge was a particularly heavy one on 15 December 1943. During the raid the Japanese commandant, Kokuba, saw the POWs running for the slit trenches, and he 'excitedly' charged out of his office waving his sword shouting, in Japanese, 'Keep calm! Keep calm! Or I will kill you!'[10] There were a further **5** bombing attacks on the bridge, on 5, 9, and 13 February 1945, on 3 April 1945 and the last one on 24 June that year.

697

In November 1944 RAF and USAAF bombers undertook **697** sorties against the railway, dropping **1,000** tons of bombs. One particular raid, on 22 April 1945, involving **40** B-24s, resulted in the destruction of **30** bridges and damage inflicted on a further **6**, in addition to which the approaches to a further **7** bridges were blown apart.[11]

Severe damage inflicted by RAF Liberator aircraft of the Strategic Air Force, Eastern Air Command in February 1945 on a bridge a few miles south of Thanbyuzayat.

When a bridge was damaged, work was started on it without delay and continued night and day until the job was completed. The average-size bridge took about a week to repair. Sometimes, if a bridge had been very badly damaged, it was found to be more expedient to erect a temporary by-pass bridge.

While the construction was in process a gang of coolies was employed unloading trains on one side of the gap and reloading trains on the other. Generally, it took about **4** hours to unload one train. The goods would be ferried across the river by small boats or carried across on a temporary footbridge.

In January 1944 Aungunang camp, which was situated close to the railway, was machine-gunned resulting in **1** man being killed and **1** wounded.

The bombers targeted, in particular, the main railway depots such as the Thailand terminus at Nong Pladuk. The POW camp was located right in the centre of sidings on which petrol and ammunition trains were parked, Japanese stores and an anti-aircraft post. The camp boundary was only **20** yards from the line.

The installations there were attacked by Allied bombers on the night of 6/7 September 1944, in a raid which lasted for **3** hours. During the raid the POWs were forced by the Japanese

– at bayonet point – to remain in their huts. One 'stick' of bombs was dropped right across the camp, killing **95** and wounding more than **300**. In the raid some petrol wagons in the sidings had been set on fire. A party of around **50** prisoners was taken by the Japanese to salvage all the undamaged wagons. There was a real chance of unexploded bombs igniting in the heat and the guards stood well back while the POWs recovered the wagons.[12]

The prisoners at Nong Pladuk were eating their evening meal on 3 December 1944 when a formation of Allied bombers was spotted approaching the camp. 'There was just enough time to take cover before it pattern-bombed the Station and sidings', recalled Lieutenant Colonel Toosey. 'The outside bomb of the pattern killed **9** P.O.W. in the centre of a slit trench area, and another bomb destroyed the Cookhouse. While rescue work was in progress two more formations approached from the opposite direction. Of these ...the outside stick in the pattern fired 2 huts and burned out a large part of the P.O.W. Hospital.'[13]

The railway at Kui Yae (186 Kilo camp) was attacked by bombers on 8 December 1944. It resulted in the death of **26** prisoners.

A party was being transported to Tampi on 8 December 1944, when the train they were on was attacked by Allied bombers. 'We dismounted from the train,' explained Driver Thomas Litherland, 'and took certain sick patients off the train and removed them down the line away from the station for safety. The Japanese guards under a Korean attached to the Japanese engineers ... forced us back to the train at the point of their rifles and we were kept there whilst the bombs were falling. The first bomb hit the engine and other bombs hit the train with the result that forty-three Prisoners of War were killed and about twelve were wounded', and **4** of the guards were also killed.[14]

Ten days later, on 18 December 1944 aircraft appeared over Tarsao camp. From that date onwards, the prisoners were not permitted to leave their huts when aircraft were heard, being told if they wanted to shelter from any bombs that might be dropped, they should hide under their bamboo beds!

One day, the prisoners at Rin Tin camp, some **181** kilometres from the railhead at Ban Pong, were marched up-country to

A bombing attack on a bridge south of the Three Pagodas Pass. (*AWM P00505.001*)

help clear the track after a train had been hit by Allied bombers: 'There were bomb craters everywhere – huge mounds of earth and rock piled up with trees shattered to matchwood. The train had been carrying Japs and POWs ...The bodies had gone by the time we arrived, but there was blood, dark and dried on twisted metal.' It took the prisoners two days to clear the wreckage and repair the track.[15]

On 3 April 1945 a lone B-24 Liberator from the United States 436th Bomb Squadron of the 7th Bomb Group bombed the wooden 'by-pass' bridge at Kanchanaburi. The bridge was badly damaged and was never rebuilt, the Japanese accepting that if they did rebuild it, it would quickly be targeted again by the Allied bombers.

It was said that at times reconnaissance aircraft were over the railway for whole days and as the Allied aircrews became more proficient the time between a train being spotted and bombers arriving over the railway became shorter and shorter. Machine-gunning was more harmful to trains than bombing. With no risk of anti-aircraft fire, the pilots could take their planes really low over the trains from where their gun crews could scarcely miss. Eventually, it reached a point that once a train had been spotted, there was not enough time for the Japanese to get the train off into a siding.

A relic of the bombing, this unexploded bomb can be seen at the railway station at Wampo, or Tham Kra Sae as it is also called.

So frequent and destructive were the attacks by the Allied bombers that all daytime movement along the railway was stopped, the trains only travelling at night. When Allied officers inspected the railway after the war they were 'impressed' by the amount of damage the bombers had inflicted on the railway, as this report makes clear: 'Nonpladuk yard seriously damaged, the water supply there wiped away, wrecked trains in the sidings, a petrol supply point burned out. In the sidings between Nonpladuk and Kanchanaburi burned out trains. The original Kanchanaburi HQ totally bombed out of existence. Tamarkan steel bridge demolished. The timber diversion bridge showing signs of having been out of action several times. Arnhirn [?] viaduct damaged. Wampo yard full of huge bomb craters. Kinsayok yard damaged. Practically all bridges on the Siam side clearly showing they had been repaired or rebuilt several times.

'On the Burma side the damage done often seemed even more impressive. The steel bridges there were mostly out. Apalon loco shed bombed out. Moulmein station near destroyed.'[16]

500

prisoners were sent to Songkurai, **12** miles south of the Three Pagodas Pass in June 1945 to build defence positions due to fears of an attack by the Anglo-Indian Fourteenth Army which was driving the Japanese forces out of Burma. There were no medical officers with the party and rations were limited to rice and a few vegetables. In the first month **18** men died.[17]

10,000

The great irony, or perhaps the word should be tragedy, of the enormous efforts and loss of life in building a railway through the jungles of western Thailand and southern Burma is that it became the means by which the Japanese Army evacuated its sick and wounded soldiers. These amounted to approximately **10,000** men.

Ultimately, the railway facilitated the Japanese Army's retreat from Burma. Many of these arrived in Thailand in conditions just as bad as those the prisoners had endured, suffering some of the same diseases and privations. Below are those Japanese units which were transported from Burma on the railway:

Period	*Unit*
Feb–Mar 1945	Isamu Division (2nd Division) – less Aoba Brigade
Feb–Jun 1945	Taka Division (5th Air Division) Complete Strength
May 1945	Hayashi HQ (HQ 15th Army)
Apr–May 1945	Matsuri (15th Division) Mixed Units
May–Jun 1945	Aoba Brigade (from 2nd Division)
May–Jul 1945	Chu Brigade (from 55th Division)
Mar–Jun 1945	1st Railway Material Supply Depot
Apr–May 1945	7th Railway Regiment
May–Jun 1945	5th Special Railway Corps
May–Aug 1945	Naval Troops

The railway is still in use today and is popular with tourists. This diesel is shown pulling into Kanchanaburi station.

Chapter 8

Counting the Cost

84 per cent of all returned Australian prisoners of war who competed mandated questionnaires stated that they had experienced or witnessed 'rape, torture, beatings or other cruelties'.[1]

100 is approximately how many locomotives were operating on the railway at the time of the Japanese surrender on 15 August 1945, along with roughly **1,250** rolling stock, not counting what was in the workshops under maintenance and repair. There were also **25** of the converted motor trucks (the Flying Kampongs) and **120** trailers. Of these, some **41** locomotives and **900** rolling stock was granted to the Thailand railways.[2]

'Never Forget'. A memorial to those who lost their lives building the railway overlooks the ground where Nieke camp used to be, now under the waters of the Vachiralongkorn dam, which was built during the 1980s.

20,260 is how many coolies were still working on the railway at the time of the surrender. Naturally, they wanted to return home, but the Japanese asked the Allied officers, who were then, quite suddenly, responsible for the railway, the Japanese and the *rŏmusha* as well as their own men, not to let them leave for the railway would cease to function in a few days without them. There was also no accommodation or food available in Thailand as a whole for such large numbers of men to suddenly appear.

Though conditions were still bad for the *rŏmusha* along the railway, there was at least a system in place which kept them housed and fed. Despite this, many did try to leave immediately after the surrender – to their misfortune. In one report, it stated that out of a party of **20** Javanese who left Neike, only **7** made it as far as Kanchanaburi, and **1** of those died within a week of his arrival.

By February 1946, there were only **1,600** native workers left, yet there were still **9,594** Japanese running the railway.[3]

After the Japanese surrender, the 9th Railway Regiment remained in theatre to repair the badly-damaged railway. When the restoration work was finished in January 1947, all officers and **267** men – classed as Japanese Surrendered Personnel, or JSP – were placed in jail in Rangoon. It is claimed they were harshly treated, receiving starvation rations of just **800** calories a day. Most of the men of both the 5th and the 9th Railway Regiments went back to Japan in October 1947.[4]

480 During the war, no Thais or Burmese were permitted to travel on the railway, the only exceptions being men and women selling fruit, etc. As soon as the war was over large numbers wanted to take advantage of the railway. The opening of the railway for civilian use offered the prospect of trade, and enterprising Indian and Chinese traders, who came from as far as Bangkok, soon made their appearance. So packed were the cars, the locals took to sitting on the roofs – and not paying. On one train **480** people managed to find space on the roofs. Even the front plates of engines were 'adorned' with passengers. It was said that even if all these freeloaders were cleared off a train before its departure, within moments women and children would be climbing back up and onto the roofs and clinging from the sides.

£1,500,000

Due to the poor, and therefore potentially dangerous, construction of the railway, and despite the efforts at repair by the Japanese, in 1947 the decision was taken by the Allied nations that the track in Burma would be pulled up and that the track in Thailand would be sold to the Thai Government for £1.5 million, the revenue raised being allocated to those countries entitled to reparations. In fact, only **10** kilometres of track from the border northwards was removed from the Burma side, the rest remaining where it lay.

Much of the other material used on the railway was returned to where it came from, though some of its infrastructure, including the Kanchanaburi bridge over the Mae Klong, remained in place. The Thais then used much of the material from the railway elsewhere in the country, the steel rails being sold as scrap metal, and the railway was closed.

The incident which led the Thai Government to close the railway came about due the visit by His Excellency The Minister of Communications who wanted to see the newly-acquired railway for himself – despite being warned that the track was in dangerously poor condition. On the trip he was accompanied by the Director of Thailand Railways and several other dignitaries. They wanted to see the famous Three Pagodas Pass.

As a safety precaution, a motor rail trolley travelled ahead of the diesel train carrying the visiting party. The trip went more or less to plan until the train moved beyond Brankasi. 'An hour after departure, the diesel engine broke down,' explained a later report. 'As it was found repairs would take hours and the motor trolley was still in sight, the whole party transferred to that trolley. Such a trolley is constructed to carry **10** to **12** men at the utmost and it seems impossible to get **22** on it but it was arranged that the Minister and higher officials took the bench seats and the other members of the party sat on the roof or just hung on.

'Running the trolley out of the curve and cutting on the approach to the bridge near 262km, the driver saw the bridge had completely disappeared, the rails only being left to bridge the gap. It was too late to do anything. Some people perceiving the situation jumped clear just before the trolley ran on the unsupported rails, went right through them and shot into the ravine (depth approximately **8.5** metres). One of the officials was killed immediately; His Excellency died after a very short time. The Director of Railways was very severely injured, several others also. Most of the party had major injuries.'[5] The 'Death Railway' had lived up to its name.

So, the line was closed shortly afterwards. However, in 1957 the State Railways of Thailand reopened a **130**-kilometre section between Nong Pladuk and Nam Tok near the former Tha Sao POW camp. This is still in use today.

The railway has become a major tourist attraction with most travellers visiting Kanchanaburi and Hellfire pass. The POW camps have been consumed by nature, as has much of the track, though its path through the jungle can still be traced in parts.

97,000 is approximately how many POWs and Asian workers were on the line at the time of the surrender. These were **32,000** POWs, **25,000** Asians from Malaya, Java and Thailand and **40,000** from Burma.

Recently-returned prisoners of war travelling by ambulance train from Sydney to Melbourne. (*AWM 115850*)

A RAAF Medical Air Evacuation Transport Unit (MAETU) nurse helps ex-prisoner of war amputees on their arrival at Singapore from Bangkok, 25 September 1945. (*AWM 119706*)

10

Following the Japanese surrender the remaining ex-prisoners in Thailand were taken back to Singapore via Bangkok. Once again, they travelled by train in the same kind of cattle trucks they had been sent in more than **2** years earlier. This time, though, it was with only **10** men in each truck.

One of those returnees was the senior Australian officer of 'F' Force, Lieutenant Colonel Kappe. According to one fellow POW, Kappe 'returned to Changi well conditioned, in fact he was fat ...He preferred not to have his face slapped by the Japanese and rarely exited his tent.'[6]

Not every prisoner endured the same privations and rank had its privileges. As the senior officer of the Australian contingent of 'F' Force, Lieutenant Colonel C. H. Kappe, on the left of this trio, was one of those officers who came in for criticism by some for avoiding confrontation with the Japanese. This photograph was taken on 20 September 1945. The other two men are Major N. Johnston, and Lieutenant Colonel Frederick Galleghan. (*AWM 117115*)

36.62

was the number of POWs who died for every **1** kilometre of track laid. Total British, Australian, Dutch and American deaths was **15,127**. It is not known with any certainty how many died

Kanchanaburi War Cemetery is the largest of the cemeteries where **6,982** men are buried.

of other nationalities. It has been estimated that this number was not less than **90,000**. This makes a total of more than **105,000**. As the sleepers were placed around **0.71** of a metre apart, this meant **1,400** sleepers per kilometre.[7] Along the full length of the railway – **414.916** kilometres – a total of **581,000** sleepers would have been laid. While it has been said that the railway cost the lives of **1** man for every sleeper, a more accurate assessment, though still shocking beyond imagining, would be closer to around **1** death for every **5** sleepers laid.

One commentator estimated that each mile of the railway was paid for with the lives of **64** Allied prisoners of war and **240** 'coolie slaves'.[8]

As might be expected, there was a disparity in the number of deaths between the Allied and the Japanese records, with the Japanese attempting to show that the totals were considerably less. The Japanese statement gives only **50,000** POWs employed among whom there were **10,000** deaths, and **100,000** coolies employed, among whom there were **30,000** deaths.[9]

Other figures have been given as follows:

Malayan civilians employed = **75,000**, number of deaths = **42,000**
Burmese civilians employed = **90,000**, number of deaths = **40,000**
Javanese civilians employed = **7,500**, number of deaths = **2,900**
Singaporean civilians employed = **5,200**, number of deaths = **500**

The totals, therefore, are **177,700** employed, resulting in **85,400** deaths.[10]

Chungkai War Cemetery holds the graves of **1,426** Commonwealth and **313** Dutch men. The war cemetery is the original burial ground started by the prisoners themselves, and the burials are mostly of men who died at the hospital.

1 The percentage of Australian officers of 'F' Force who died during the construction of the railway, whereas the death rate in 'F' Force as a whole was **44** per cent. The death rate among British officers of 'F' Force was between **2** and **2.5** per cent.[11] As previously mentioned, there were numerous complaints made by other ranks in some, but certainly not all, camps throughout the length of the railway that their officers – most of whom were not made to work by the Japanese – experienced a comparatively comfortable existence while the men they were responsible for were worked and starved to death. This is reflected in these statistics.

3270 is how many men of 'H' Force died, as stated in the 'H' Force report written by Lieutenant Colonel R.A. Humphries on 26 May 1944. The statistics, though not as pronounced as those relating to 'F' Force, do show a similar correlation between the mortality of officers and those of the other ranks. Only **6.27** per cent of officers died while **26.83** per cent of Australian other ranks and **37.30** per cent of British other ranks succumbed.[12]

144 is how many cemeteries were found by an Allied War Graves Commission survey party which was given the task of finding and exhuming the remains of the POWs who had died along the railway. This party included Allied officers, former POWs and a Japanese translator. The party set off from Ban Pong on 22 September 1945 and travelled by train to Thanbyuzayat, arriving there on 24 September. From there the party worked back towards Thailand over the course of two weeks, encountering Japanese units, some of whom helped them, others who had not

A photograph of Tanbaya hospital cemetery in October 1945. The cross is a memorial to **6** officers and **757** other ranks who died at Tanbaya. (*AWM P01910.013*)

formally surrendered, proving less amenable. In total, the party located the graves of **10,549** men buried in **144** cemeteries. Remarkably, only **52** of the graves the party had set out to find remained undiscovered.[13]

When gathering together all the bodies at the ex-POW Headquarters in Bangkok, all available were checked and a card index was made giving, where possible, the following information on each dead man:

Number
Rank
Name
Unit
Date of Death
Cause of Death
Place of Burial
Grave Number

From the British card index an alphabetical nominal roll was compiled. All the records from which the roll was compiled were handed over to the Officer Commanding, Graves Registration Unit.[14]

Chungkai Cemetery as it appeared in September 1945. At the time there were two cemeteries, one with **1,500** graves and one with **168** graves.

Thanbyuzayat War Cemetery is where **3,149** Commonwealth and **621** Dutch are buried from the Burmese section of the railway. (*Courtesy Phyo WP*)

12,493

Is the total number of prisoners of war buried at Chungkai, Kanchanaburi and Thanbyuzayat cemeteries. Of this number **6,540** are British, **2,830** are Dutch, **2,710** are Australian. There are also **220** Malayan, **33** Indian, **5** New Zealand, **2** Canadian, **2** Burmese and another **151** of unknown nationality.[15]

The remains from all the graves along the southern section of railway as far as Neike are in the Kanchanaburi War Cemetery and included in this number are some **300** men who died (most from a cholera epidemic in May/June 1943) at Nieke camp who were cremated, and their ashes now lie in two graves in the cemetery. The remains of the bodies recovered from the camp cemeteries in Burma now rest at Thanbyuzayat War Cemetery in Myanmar. There, **3,149** Commonwealth and **621** Dutch former POWs lie in peace.

The bodies of the Americans who died during captivity were repatriated.

2

Only **2** Japanese general officers were found guilty of war crimes relating to the death and suffering of the men who worked on the railway, of these just **1** received the death sentence with the other receiving a prison sentence. Of officers of field rank, all **11** who were indicted were found guilty, of whom **5** received death sentences. Of the **37** company level officers, **33** were found guilty, with **12** receiving the death sentence. Only **1** of these was a Japanese railway engineer – Captain Eiji Hirota, who was hanged – all the others were camp officers.

Nieke, Burma, October 1945. Group of Japanese war crimes suspects, formerly guards at POW camps await their fate. (*AWM P01910.004*)

With regards to NCOs, **23** were indicted, **20** were found guilty and **4** were sentenced to death. Just **12** ordinary privates were indicted and while all were found guilty only **1** was given the death sentence. The last category was the Korean and other civilian auxiliaries such as interpreters. These formed the second largest group, with **35** being indicted, **33** found guilty and **9** receiving death sentences.[16]

'F' Force suffered the most heavily of all those sent to work on the railway but only **8** of its Japanese and Korean guards were put on trial. Of these **4** received jail terms of between **3** and **5** years. The other **4** – Captains Muruyama Hajime and Fukuda Tsuneo, as well as the Korean, Toyoyama Kisei, and Lieutenant Abe Hiroshi were sentenced to death. However, the evidence before the court did not sufficiently establish that the accused actually caused the death of any POW, or participated in such brutality as would justify the imposition of the death penalty. The conclusion was, therefore, that all the sentences would stand, but that the death sentences would be commuted. This resulted in life imprisonment for Tsuneo and Kisei, and **15** years each for Hajime and Abe Hiroshi. Ishimoto Eishin was given the lightest sentence of all, just **18** months.[17]

Detailed affidavits were submitted by many of the prisoners upon their release from the prison camps regarding the treatment they had received at the hands of the Japanese. Often the rank and file prisoners did not know the name of the Japanese or Korean about whom they were reporting, using only the nicknames the POWs had given them. One such example is a Japanese NCO who was known to the prisoners as 'The Tiger'. However, the senior British, Dutch or Australian officers did know the names of the camp commanders which helped them to be accurately identified. So, 'The Tiger' was named by Lieutenant Colonel C. E. Mackellar as Sergeant Hiramatsu Ajitaro, who wrote of the latter's 'outbursts of sadistic mania' and his driving sick prisoners to work by 'armed force' and of 'beating sick men in [a] hospital lorry during evacuation of sick'.[18] He was sentenced to death by hanging which was later commuted to life imprisonment.[19]

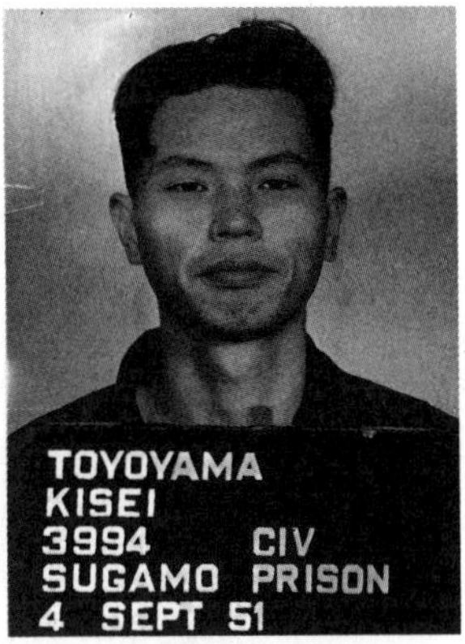

Civilian Toyoyama Kisei was sentenced to death by hanging, it being noted at his trial for war crimes that 'he was noted for his continuous beating of officers and men, often using a steel shaft of a golf club as a weapon'.

Possibly one of the most sadistic of the Japanese officers was Major Totaro Mizutani, who was accused of three separate crimes. First, inhumane treatment of prisoners of war who were working on the Burma Railway, forcing sick prisoners to march more than **200** miles to work while failing to provide adequate food and medical supplies for them. Of roughly **2,000** prisoners in his charge, it was alleged that **570** died. Second, Mizutani was accused of ill treatment of a Burmese civilian who had begged

Another of the defendants at the War Crimes Trials held in Singapore on 12–13, 19 and 22 August 1946, was 'The Tiger', Hiramatsu Ajitaro.

him for food; the Japanese major allegedly burned the victim with a flaming piece of wood.

Third, Mizutani was charged with shooting and killing Fusilier L.W. Wanty, a British prisoner, when he was caught wandering outside his sleeping quarters after lights out.

The incident involving Wanty occurred on 31 December 1944. That night, shortly after 'lights out' at approximately 23.45 hours, Len Wanty of the Royal Northumberland Fusiliers, was stopped by a Korean guard when he was trying to cross from the work camp to the hospital. After being interrogated by the Koreans it was agreed Wanty should be released. At this point Major Mitzuani appeared on the scene and asked what was happening. When the major learned that Wanty had been trying to reach the hospital after lights out, he immediately said: 'There is no need for further enquiry, this man must be shot.' He ordered one of the Koreans to kill Wanty. The guard refused, so Mitzuani slapped him in the face three times, took his rifle from him. He told Wanty to walk

Objects from the railway are displayed in both Japan and Britain. At the Yasukuni Shrine in Tokyo, is the locomotive which was the first to cross into Burma from Thailand at the ceremony on the joining of the two ends of the line – number C5631. (*Courtesy LERK*)

towards the fence surrounding the camp. Mitzuani walked up behind the fusilier and shot him in the back. Wanty fell down and died. [20] Mizutani was sentenced to death by hanging.

9

is how many men of 'H' Force were Mentioned in Despatches by its commander, Lieutenant Colonel Humphries. In addition, he recommended three men for the award of the MBE, including Padre L.T. Marsden, while one officer, Major K.J. Fagan, was recommended for the OBE.

76.50

In pounds sterling, this is how much the British POWs who worked on the railway initially received in compensation for all they had endured. This was composed of money from Japanese assets in Axis and neutral countries transferred to the International Committee of the Red Cross. The UK's share of **£1,636,281** produced a payment of **£25** per prisoner. In addition to this amount Her Majesty's Government decided to use the proceeds of Japanese assets in the UK, retained under Article 14 of the 1951 Treaty of San Francisco, to make ex-gratia payments to British ex-POWs and civilian internees, amounting to **£48.50** per head. Her Majesty's Government also received from the Thai Government **£174,871** from the sale of the railway, giving a further **£3** per POW and bringing the maximum total of payment to **£76.50**. This amount was distributed mainly in 1952–6 to some **50,000** ex-POWs.

The Dutch government received 1 million guilders, the equivalent of **616,490** US dollars as a compensation for the **17,399** POWs of whom **2,899** died building the railway. Claimants were requested to send a postcard to the Ministry of Foreign Affairs with their personal data and the names of the POW camps where they had been held captive. A total of **61,75** guilders, or **38** US dollars, was paid to each successful claimant.

However, in 1998, the UK Government agreed to pay all surviving Far East Prisoners of War **£10,000**.

41

This is the percentage of those former POWs who suffered psychiatric problems in the years after the war who were treated at the Queen Mary's Hospital, Roehampton between 1946 and

1968. This military hospital took the lead in providing care for Far East Prisoners of War. During this period, hundreds of POWs were treated, most of whom continued to suffer from recurrent malaria and dysentery caused by intestinal parasites.

When Roehampton ceased to function as a military hospital, the Liverpool School of Tropical Medicine became the official national screening and treatment centre. It continued in this role until the end of the twentieth century, by which time numbers had declined to just single figures.

In Britain a 30-metre stretch of the railway constructed from original rails and sleepers can be seen at the National Memorial Arboretum, at Alrewas, near Lichfield, Staffordshire.

Notes

Chapter 1: The Plan

1. TNA HW 12/278.
2. TNA FO 628/67. The term 'nail crew' probably refers to the spike teams, as mentioned later.
3. Clifford Kinvig, *River Kwai Railway, The Story of the Burma-Siam Railroad* (Brassey's, London, 1992), pp. 42 & 45.
4. Kazuo Tamayama, *Building the Burma-Thailand Railway 1942-43, An Epic of World War II* (The World War II Remembrance Group, Japan, 2004), p. x.
5. TNA WO 203/6325.
6. TNA FO 628/67.
7. TNA WO 325/157.
8. TNA WO 203/6325.
9. Lionel Wigmore, *Australia in the War of 1939–1945, Volume IV – The Japanese Thrust, Part III – Prisoners of the Japanese* (Australian War Memorial, Canberra, 1957), p. 382.
10. Supplement to *The London Gazette*, 13 February 1942, Numb. 35456, p. 749.
11. TNA WO 325/117.
12. E. E. Dunlop, *The War Diaries of Weary Dunlop, Java and the Burma-Thailand Railway 1942-1945* (Penguin, Harmondsworth, 1986), p. 244.
13. TNA WO 203/5823.
14. TNA WO 203/6325.
15. Arthur Godman, *The Will to Survive* (Spellmount, Staplehurst, 2002), p. 103.
16. http://www.mansell.com/POW_resources/camplists/death_rr/dutch_view_death_railway.html.
17. John Grehan, *Medical Officers on the Infamous Burma Railway, Accounts of Life, Death & War Crimes By Those Who Were There* (Frontline, Barnsley, 2022), p. 7.
18. Rory Laird, *From Shanghai to the Burma Railway, The Memoirs & Letters of Richard Laird, A Japanese Prisoner of War* (Pen & Sword, Barnsley, 2020), p. 88.
19. TNA WO 235/963.
20. Stanley Wood-Higgs, *Bamboo and Barbed Wire* (Roman Press, Bournemouth, 1988), p. 59.
21. Hugh V. Clarke, *A Life For Every Sleeper: A Pictorial Record of the Burma-Thailand Railway* (Allan & Unwin, Sydney, 1986), p. 22.
22. Rowland Perry, *Red Lead – The Naval Cat with Nine Lives* (Allen and Unwin, Sydney, 2020).
23. TNA WO 325/117.
24. TNA WO 203/6325.
25. Quoted in Kazunori Hashimoto, *Constructing the Burma-Thailand Railway: The War Crimes Trials and the Shaping of an Episode of WWII* (Department of History SOAS, University of London, 2022), pp. 139–40.

26. TNA WO 235/963.

Chapter 2: The Work Begins

1. Dunlop, p. 208.
2. TNA FO 371/112291.
3. Paul Kratoska, *The Thailand-Burma Railway, 1942-1946: Documents and Selected Writings* (Routledge, Abingdon-on-Thames, 2005), p. 42.
4. AWM 54, 1010/3/10.
5. Hilary Custance Green (ed.), *Surviving the Death Railway, A POW's Memoir and Letters from Home* (Pen & Sword, Barnsley, 2016), pp. 84–5.
6. www.230battalion.org.au.
7. TNA, WO 235/963.
8. James Bradley, *Cyril Wild, The Tall Man Who Never Slept* (Woodfield Publishing, Bognor Regis, 1997), p. 62.
9. John Coast, *Railroad of Death: The Original, Classic Account of the 'River Kwai' Railway* (Hyperon, London, 1946), p. 104.
10. TWA WO 235/963.
11. Ibid.
12. Ernest Gordon, *Through the Valley of the Kwai* (Harper & Row, London, 1962), p. 70
13. Tamayama, p. 6.
14. Peter N. Davies, *The Man behind the Bridge: Colonel Toosey and the River Kwai* (Athlone, London, 1991), p. 108.
15. TNA WO 325/117.
16. Ian Denys Peek, *One Fourteenth of an Elephant, A Memoir of Life and Death on the Burma-Thailand Railway* (Doubleday, London, 2004), p. 169.
17. Peter Fyans, *Conjuror on the Kwai, The Incredible Life of Fergus Anckorn* (Pen & Sword, Barnsley, 2011), pp. 125–6.
18. Gavan McCormack and Hank Nelson (eds), *The Burma-Thailand Railway: Memory and History* (Allen & Unwin, Sidney, 1993), p. 40.
19. Tamayama, p. VIII.
20. A. A. Apthorpe, *The British Sumatra Battalion* (Book Guild, Lewes, 1988), p. 98.
21. R. H. Whitecross, *Slaves of the Son of Heaven, A Personal Account of an Australian POW 1942-1945* (Simon & Schuster, London, 2001), p. 90.
22. Harry Howarth, *Where Fate Leads* (Ross Anderson, Bolton, 1983), p. 200.
23. Tamayama, pp. 35–6.
24. 'Of elephants and men' in McCormack and Nelson, p. 40.
25. TNA WO 235/963.
26. TNA WO 325/18.
27. anzacportal.dva.gov.au/resources/stolen-years-australian-prisoners-war.
28. Jeffery English, *One For Every Sleeper, The Japanese Death Railway through Thailand* (Robert Hale, London, 1989), p. 141.
29. S. Dawson. *Memoirs of experiences on the Thai/Burma Railway*, 1946. IWM 95/911, p. 161.
30. Dunlop, p. 240.
31. Custance Green, pp. 106–07.
32. TNA WO 325/90, Japanese Official Report.
33. TNA WO 325/90.
34. Grehan, p. 79.

35. Ibid., p. 18.
36. Tamayama, p. 58.
37. www.230battalion.org.au.
38. TNA WO 311/547.
39. Ibid.
40. Ibid.

Chapter 3: Life in the Camps

1. The full list can be found in TNA WO 325/157.
2. Kratoska, p. 56.
3. TNA WO 325/157.
4. Eric Lomax, *The Railway Man* (Vantage, London, 1996), pp. 119–20.
5. Colonel Cary Owtram OBE, *1000 Days on the River Kwai, The Secret Diary of a British Camp Commandant* (Pen & Sword, Barnsley, 2017), pp. 36–7.
6. Wigmore, p. 560.
7. Kratoska, pp. 72–3.
8. Stan Arneil, *One Man's War* (Alternative Press, Sydney, 1980), pp. 130 & 133.
9. TNA WO 235/963.
10. Ibid.
11. Jonathan Moffatt and Audrey Holmes McCormick, *Moon Over Malaya, The 2nd Argylls and Plymouth Royal Marines in Malaya and Singapore* (The History Press, Stroud, 2014), p. 226.
12. Kratoska, p. 58.
13. Gordon, p. 75.
14. Also, and more often, spelt 'qualies', also 'kwalis' or 'kualis'.
15. Frank Foster, 'Railway of Death', *The Listener*, 15 November 1945, p. 555.
16. TNA WO 235/963.
17. TNA WO 208/3758.
18. Wigmore, p. 557.
19. Russell Braddon, *The Naked Island* (Doubleday, New York, 1953), p. 205.
20. Dunlop, p. 252.
21. From Appendix C of *The V Report*, UK Red Cross Archives, ACC 0033 A/3 reproduced in Geoff Gill and Meg Parkes, *Burma Railway Medicine, Disease, Death and Survival on the Thai-Burma Railway 1942-1945* (Palatine, Lancaster, 2017), pp. 205–8.
22. TNA WO 235/963.
23. Geoffrey Pharaoh Adams, *No Time For Geishas* (Lee Cooper, London, 1973), pp. 90–107.
24. TNA WO 203//6325.
25. Gordon, p. 68.
26. R. F. Oakes, 'Work and be happy', AWM MSS 1037, quoted on anzacportal.dva.gov.au.
27. Robert S. La Forte and Ronald E. Marcello, *Building the Death Railway: The Ordeal of American POWS in Burma, 1942-1945* (Rowman & Littlefield, 1993), p. 172.
28. Otto Kreeff (trans. Webb, John and Crombie, Netteke), *Burma Railway, A Visual Recollection* (Museum Bronbeck, 2008) p. 50.
29. Braddon, p. 221.
30. TNA WO 208/1925.
31. Godman, p. 115.

32. Pattie Wright, *The Men of the Line: Stories of the Thai-Burma Railway Survivors* (Miegunyah Press, Melbourne, 2008), p. 163.
33. TNA WO 235/1034.
34. Allan S. Walker, *Australia in the War of 1939–1945, Series Five, Medical, Volume II, Middle East and Far East*, (Australian War Memorial, Canberra, 1962), p. 579.
35. TNA WO 235/963.
36. Wigmore, p. 577.
37. TNA WO 235/963.
38. Ibid.
39. Rod Beattie, 'An update on research into and exploration along the Thailand-Burma Railway', www.shbss.nl.
40. TNA WO 325/157.
41. Robert Hardie, *The Burma-Siam Railway, The secret diary of Dr Robert Hardie 1943-45* (Imperial War Museum, London, 1983), p. 149.
42. TNA WO 325/35, Report by Lt. Col. P.J.D. Toosey on Malay and Thailand Prisoner of War Camps.
43. TNA WO 235/963.
44. AWM 54 554/5/1.
45. Beattie, 'An update on research into and exploration along the Thailand-Burma Railway'.
46. TNA WO 235/963.
47. Tamayama, pp. 72–3.
48. Ibid., p. 77.
49. Wigmore, p. 552.
50. Ibid., p. 563.
51. TNA WO 311/547.
52. TNA WO 235/1034.
53. Ibid.
54. AWM 54 554/5/1.
55. TNA FO 628/67.
56. Rod Beattie, *The Death Railway – A Brief History of The Thailand-Burma Railway* (T.B.R.C. Kanchanaburi, 2015), p. 100.
57. Kratoska, p. 68.
58. Harold A. Skinner, *'Guest' of the Imperial Japanese Army 1941-45* (Privately published, Littlehampton, 1993), p. 12.
59. Peek, p. 126.
60. John Durnford, *Branch Line to Burma* (Four Square, London, 1966).
61. TNA WO 235/963.
62. Private Papers of R. J. Godber, IWM Catalogue number Documents.20966.

Chapter 4: Disease and Death

1. TNA WO 325/157.
2. G. V. Gill, *Coping with Crisis: Medicine and Disease on the Burma Railway 1942 -1945.* (Doctoral thesis, University of Liverpool, 2009), p. 124.
3. Quoted, unsourced, in Kratoska, p. 107.
4. L. L. Baynes, *Kept: the Other Side of Tenko* (Book Guild, Lewes, 1984), p. 89.
5. TNA WO208/3258, Medical Report on F Force by Lt. Col. Huston', p. 16.

6. Peter Brune, *Descent into Hell, The Fall of Singapore – Pudu and Changi – The Thai-Burma Railway* (Allen & Unwin, London, 2014), p. 604.
7. Stanley S. Pavillard, *Bamboo Doctor* (Macmillan, London, 1960), pp. 151–2.
8. Gill and Parkes, p. 73.
9. Howarth, pp. 190–1.
10. Pavillard, p. 43.
11. TNA WO 325/16.
12. Peek, pp. 173–4.
13. English, p. 148.
14. war-experience.org/events/the-thaiburma-railroad.
15. G. Freed and P. B. Stringer. *Comparative mortality experience 1946-1963 among former Australian prisoners of war of the Japanese* (Repatriation Dept, Central Medical Research Advisory Committee, Melbourne, Australia, 1968).
16. F. Whalley. IWM Catalogue number, Documents.7797.
17. E. S. Benfield, unpublished typescript, *The rising sun on my back a personal account of war, 1939-1945*, IWM Catalogue number, LBY K. 95 / 2303.
18. TNA WO 325/117.
19. TNA WO 325/90.
20. Grehan, p. 57.
21. Walker, p. 600.
22. Grehan, pp. 126–7.
23. Report on Tarsau Base Hospital, AWM 54 554/5/1.
24. G.V. Gill, p. 128.
25. TNA WO 325/159.
26. anzacportal.dva.gov.au.
27. Bill Reed with Mitch Peeke, *Lost Souls of the River Kwai, Experiences of a British Soldier on the Railway of Death* (Pen & Sword, Barnsley, 2004), p. 84.
28. Braddon, p. 228.
29. 2/4th Machine Gun Battalion, 2nd4thmgb.com.au.
30. TNA WO 235/867.
31. Quoted in G.V. Gill, p. 115.
32. AWM 54 554/5/1.
33. TNA WO 325/117.
34. TNA WO 325/159.
35. Hardie, p. 104.

Chapter 5: Escape

1. I. Morrison, *Grandfather Longlegs* (Faber & Faber, London, 1947), p. 205.
2. See, Philip Davies. *Lost Warriors – Seagrim and Pagani of Burma: The last great untold story of WWII* (Atlantic Publishing, 2017).
3. Report prepared by Lieutenant Colonel F. J. Dillon, AWM PR88/095.
4. TNA WO 235/963.
5. Dunlop, p. 227.
6. AWM 54 1010/4/65.
7. Owtram, p. 24.
8. Wigmore, p. 550.
9. Ibid.

10. James Bradley, *Towards the Setting Sun, An Escape from the Thailand-Burma Railway, 1943* (J.M.L. Fuller, Wellington, 1982), p. 72.
11. Kratoska, pp. 288–90. See also James Bradley's own account, *Towards the Setting Sun*, pp. 53, & 67–98.
12. Kenneth Adams, *Healing in Hell, The Memoirs of a Far Eastern POW Medic* (Pen & Sword, Barnsley, 2011), p. 95.
13. Peter Jackson, *Sacrifice, Captivity & Escape, The Remarkable Memoirs of a Japanese POW* (Pen & Sword, Barnsley, 2012), pp. 93–127.
14. TNA WO 230/6325.
15. Reed and Peeke, pp. 76–7.
16. Toosey Journal, TNA WO 325/35.
17. TNA WO 235/963, Judge Advocate General's Office: War Crimes Case Files, Second World War.
18. Rowley Richards and Marcia McEwan, *The Survival Factor* (Costello, Tunbridge Wells, 1989), pp. 111–12.

Chapter 6: Construction and Completion

1. TNA FO 628/67.
2. Tamayama, p. 69.
3. Clarke, pp. 60–1.
4. Gavan Daws, *Prisoners of the Japanese* (Simon & Schuster, London, 2006), p. 217.
5. Kinvig, p. 139.
6. TNA FO 628/67.
7. Bradley, *Towards the Setting Sun*, p. 53.
8. Daws, p. 217.
9. Tamayama, p. x.
10. Daws, p. 217.
11. Wigmore, p. 585.
12. Sears A. Eldredge, *Captive Audiences/Captive Performers, Music and Theatre as Strategies for Survival on the Thailand-Burma Railway 1942-1945*, DigitalCommons@ Macalaster College, 2014, p. 50.
13. TNA WO 203/6325.
14. www.cofepow.org.uk/armed-forces-stories-list/the-mergui-road-burma.
15. TNA 325/157.
16. Another account claims the number that died was 284, TNA WO 235/963.

Chapter 7: Running the Railway

1. TNA FO 628/67.
2. Ibid.
3. Other sources state that 52 came from Japan, 53 from Malaya, 30 from Burma and 7 from Java, see anzacportal.dva.gov.au.
4. Reed and Peeke, pp. 78–9.
5. TNA WO 203/6325.
6. Beattie, *The Death Railway*, p. 133.
7. TNA WO 325/17.
8. TNA WO 203/6325.
9. AWM, 54 554/2/1C.

10. Albert Coates and Newman Rosenthal, *The Albert Coates Story, The Will that Found the Way*, Hyland House, Melbourne, 1977, p. 154.
11. Kinvig, pp. 81–2.
12. TNA WO 235/963.
13. AWM 54 554/2/1C.
14. TNA WO 235/918.
15. Reg Twigg, *Survivor on the River Kwai, The Incredible Story of Life on the Burma Railway*, Viking, London, 2013, pp. 225–6.
16. TNA FO 628/67.
17. Wigmore, p. 590.

Chapter 8: Counting the Cost

1. 'Commemorating Australian Prisoners Of War On The Burma–Thailand Railway: Wartime Snapshots No.12', Anzac Portal.
2. TNA FO 628/67.
3. Ibid.
4. Tamayama, p. 99.
5. TNA FO 628/67.
6. 2nd4thmgb.com.au.
7. Tamayama, p. VIII.
8. Lord Russell of Liverpool, *The Knights of Bushido, A History of Japanese War Crimes During World War II* (Frontline, Barnsley, 2016), p. 95.
9. TNA FO 371/112291, 'Paper on Siam-Burma Railway', pp. 2–3.
10. mansell.com/POW resources/camplists/death.
11. McCormack and Nelson, p. 101.
12. TNA WO 325/17.
13. anzacportal.dva.gov.au.
14. TNA WO 361/2237.
15. *Hellfire Pass Memorial Thailand-Burma Railway* (Australian-Thai Chamber of Commerce, Bangkok, 1999), p. 15.
16. McCormack and Nelson, p. 133.
17. Grehan, pp. 204–05.
18. TNA WO 235/918.
19. ICC Legal Tools Database.
20. TNA WO 311/547.

Source Information

National Archives, Kew

FO 371/112291, Paper on Siam-Burma railway.

FO 628/67, History of the construction by the Japanese of the Siam-Burma Railway during the Second World War.

HW 12/278, Decrypts of intercepted diplomatic communications.

WO 203/5823, SEATIC Publication No.246, *Burma-Siam Railway*, 8 October 1946.

WO 203/6325, Burma – Siam railway: history compiled by Canadian Intelligence Corps.

WO 208/1925, Building of the Burma-Thailand railway.

WO 208/3258, Medical Report on F Force by Lt. Col. Huston.

WO 235/867, Judge Advocate General's Office War Crimes Case Files.

WO 235/918, Judge Advocate General's Office War Crimes Case Files

WO 235/963, Judge Advocate General's Office War Crimes Case Files.

WO 235/1034, Judge Advocate General's Office War Crimes Case Files.

WO 311/547, Burma-Siam Railway, Tamuang Camp: killing and ill-treatment of British POWs

WO 325/16, Burma-Siam Railway `F' Force: account of events and war crimes against POWs working on railway.

WO 325/17, Burma-Siam Railway Force H: war crimes against POWs working on railway.

WO 325/35, Report by Lt. Col. P.J.D. Toosey on Malay and Thailand Prisoner of War Camps.

WO 325/90, Employment of POWs on Burma-Siam Railway: part 2 of report by Japanese Government

WO 325/117 Burma-Siam Railway, Thanbyuzayat Camp: statements on conditions and ill treatment of POWs and coolies.

WO 325/157, Burma/Siam Railway: charges against Japanese high commanders.

WO 325/159, Hospital camps on the Burma/Siam Railway, 1943-1945.

WO 361/2237, Prisoners of war, Far East: Thailand-Burma Railway camps; report of graves and deaths, statistics of British, Australian, American and Dutch personnel in Thailand.

Australian War Memorial

AWM 54 554/2/1C, 8th Division in Captivity – 'A' Force (Burma).

AWM 54 554/5/1, POW Camps, Thailand, Report on Kinsayok Camp and Hospital and Tarsau Base Hospital, 1943-1944.

AWM 54, 1010/3/10, War Crimes and Trials – Transcripts of Evidence.

AWM 54 1010/4/65, War Crimes and Trials – Affidavits and Sworn Statements.

AWM MSS 1037, R. F. Oakes, 'Work and be happy'.

AWM PR88/095, Report prepared by Lieutenant Colonel F J Dillon.

Imperial War Museum

E. S. Benfield, unpublished typescript, *The rising sun on my back a personal account of war, 1939-1945*, Catalogue number, LBY K. 95 / 2303.

R. J. Godber, private papers, Catalogue number Documents.20966.

F. Whalley, private papers, Catalogue number, Documents.7797.

Published books

Adams, Geoffrey Pharaoh, *No Time For Geishas* (Lee Cooper, London, 1973).

Arneil, Stan, *One Man's War* (Alternative Press, Sydney, 1980).

Baynes, L.L., *Kept: the Other Side of Tenko* (Book Guild, Lewes, 1984).

Beattie, Rod, *The Death Railway – A Brief History of The Thailand-Burma Railway* (T.B.R.C. Kanchanaburi, 2015).

Braddon, Russell, *The Naked Island* (Doubleday, New York, 1953).

Bradley, James, *Towards the Setting Sun, An Escape from the Thailand-Burma Railway, 1943* (J.M.L. Fuller, Wellington, 1982).

—, *Cyril Wild, The Tall Man Who Never Slept* (Woodfield Publishing, Bognor Regis, 1997).

Brune, Peter, *Descent into Hell, The Fall of Singapore – Pudu and Changi – The Thai-Burma Railway* (Allen & Unwin, London, 2014).

Clarke, Hugh V., *A Life For Every Sleeper: A Pictorial Record of the Burma-Thailand Railway* (Allan & Unwin, Sydney, 1986).

Coast, John, *Railroad of Death: The Original, Classic Account of the 'River Kwai' Railway* (Hyperon, London, 1946).

Coates, Albert, and Rosenthal, Newman, *The Albert Coates Story, The Will that Found the Way*, Hyland House, Melbourne, 1977.

Davies, Peter N., *The Man behind the Bridge: Colonel Toosey and the River Kwai* (Athlone, London, 1991).

Davies, Philip, *Lost Warriors – Seagrim and Pagani of Burma: The last great untold story of WWII* (Atlantic Publishing, 2017).

Daws, Gavan, *Prisoners of the Japanese* (Simon & Schuster, London, 2006).

Dunlop, E. E., *The War Diaries of Weary Dunlop, Java and the Burma-Thailand Railway 1942-1945* (Penguin, Harmondsworth, 1986).

Durnford, John, *Branch Line to Burma* (Four Square, London, 1966).

English, Jeffery, *One For Every Sleeper, The Japanese Death Railway through Thailand* (Robert Hale, London, 1989).

Gill, Geoff and Parkes, Meg, *Burma Railway Medicine, Disease, Death and Survival on the Thai-Burma Railway 1942-1945* (Palatine, Lancaster, 2017).

Godman, Arthur, *The Will to Survive* (Spellmount, Staplehurst, 2002).

Gordon, Ernest, *Through the Valley of the Kwai* (Harper & Row, London, 1962).

Green, Hilary Custance (ed.), *Surviving the Death Railway, A POW's Memoir and Letters from Home* (Pen & Sword, Barnsley, 2016).

Grehan, John, *Medical Officers on the Infamous Burma Railway, Accounts of Life, Death & War Crimes By Those Who Were There* (Frontline, Barnsley, 2022).

Hellfire Pass Memorial Thailand-Burma Railway (Australian-Thai Chamber of Commerce, Bangkok, 1999).

Howarth, Harry, *Where Fate Leads* (Ross Anderson, Bolton, 1983).

Kinvig, Clifford, *River Kwai Railway, The Story of the Burma-Siam Railroad* (Brassey's, London, 1992).

Kratoska, Paul, *The Thailand-Burma Railway, 1942-1946: Documents and Selected Writings* (Routledge, Abingdon-on-Thames, 2005).
Kreeff, Otto [trans. Webb, John and Crombie, Netteke], *Burma Railway, A Visual Recollection* (Museum Bronbeck, 2008).
La Forte, Robert S. and Marcello, Ronald E., *Building the Death Railway: The Ordeal of American POWS in Burma, 1942-1945* (Rowman & Littlefield, 1993).
Laird, Rory, *From Shanghai to the Burma Railway, The Memoirs & Letters of Richard Laird, A Japanese Prisoner of War* (Pen & Sword, Barnsley, 2020).
Lomax, Eric, *The Railway Man* (Vantage, London, 1996).
McCormack, Gavan and Nelson, Hank [eds.], *The Burma-Thailand Railway: Memory and History* (Allen & Unwin, Sidney, 1993).
Moffatt, Jonathan and McCormick, Audrey Holmes, *Moon Over Malaya, The 2nd Argylls and Plymouth Royal Marines in Malaya and Singapore* (The History Press, Stroud, 2014).
Morrison, I., *Grandfather Longlegs* (Faber & Faber, London, 1947).
Owtram, Colonel Cary, OBE, *1000 Days on the River Kwai, The Secret Diary of a British Camp Commandant* (Pen & Sword, Barnsley, 2017).
Pavillard, Stanley S., *Bamboo Doctor* (Macmillan, London, 1960).
Perry, Rowland, *Red Lead – The Naval Cat with Nine Lives* (Allen and Unwin, Sydney, 2020).
Reed, Bill with Peeke, Mitch, *Lost Souls of the River Kwai, Experiences of a British Soldier on the Railway of Death* (Pen & Sword, Barnsley, 2004).
Russell, Lord of Liverpool, *The Knights of Bushido, A History of Japanese War Crimes During World War II* (Frontline, Barnsley, 2016).
Skinner, Harold A., *'Guest' of the Imperial Japanese Army 1941-45* (Privately published, Littlehampton, 1993).
Tamayama, Kazuo, *Building the Burma-Thailand Railway 1942-43, An Epic of World War II* (The World War II Remembrance Group, Japan, 2004).
Twigg, Reg, *Survivor on the River Kwai, The Incredible Story of Life on the Burma Railway,* Viking, London, 2013.
Walker, Allan S., *Australia in the War of 1939–1945, Series Five, Medical, Volume II, Middle East and Far East,* (Australian War Memorial, Canberra, 1962).
Whitecross, R.H., *Slaves of the Son of Heaven, A Personal Account of an Australian POW 1942-1945* (Simon & Schuster, London, 2001).
Wigmore, Lionel, *Australia in the War of 1939–1945, Volume IV – The Japanese Thrust, Part III – Prisoners of the Japanese* (Australian War Memorial, Canberra, 1957).
Wood-Higgs, Stanley, *Bamboo and Barbed Wire* (Roman Press, Bournemouth, 1988).
Wright, Pattie, *The Men of the Line: Stories of the Thai-Burma Railway Survivors* (Miegunyah Press, Melbourne, 2008).

Internet

2/4th Machine Gun Battalion, 2nd4thmgb.com.au.
www.230battalion.org.au.
anzacportal.dva.gov.au.
www.cofepow.org.uk/armed-forces-stories-list/the-mergui-road-burma.
Sears A. Eldredge, *Captive Audiences/Captive Performers, Music and Theatre as Strategies for Survival on the Thailand-Burma Railway 1942-1945*, DigitalCommons@Macalaster College, 2014.
ICC Legal Tools Database.

mansell.com/POW_resources/camplists/death.
G. Freed & P.B., Stringer. *Comparative mortality experience 1946-1963 among former Australian prisoners of war of the Japanese* (Repatriation Dept, Central Medical Research Advisory Committee, Melbourne, Australia, 1968).
G.V. Gill, *Coping with Crisis Medicine and disease on the Burma Railway 1942 -1945.* (Doctoral thesis, University of Liverpool, 2009).
Hashimoto, Kazunori, *Constructing the Burma-Thailand Railway: The War Crimes Trials and the Shaping of an Episode of WWII* (Department of History SOAS, University of London, 2022).
http://www.mansell.com/POW_resources/camplists/death_rr/dutch_view_death_railway.html.
Rod Beattie, 'An update on research into and exploration along the Thailand-Burma Railway', www.shbss.nl.
war-experience.org/events/the-thaiburma-railroad.

Periodicals

The Listener.
The London Gazette.